THE FOURTH EDITION

The Collectors Encyclopedia of

FIESTA

With Harlequin and Riviera

by
Sharon & Bob Huxford

COLLECTOR BOOKS
A Division of Schroeder Publishing Co., Inc.

P.O. BOX 3009   PADUCAH, KENTUCKY   42001

The current values in this book should be used only as a guide. They are not intended to set prices which vary from one section of the country to another. Auction prices as well as dealer prices vary greatly and are affected by condition as well as demand. Neither the Author nor the Publisher assumes responsibility for any losses that might be incurred as a result of consulting this guide.

Additional copies of this book may be ordered from:

COLLECTOR BOOKS
P.O. Box 3009
Paducah, Kentucky   42001
or
The authors: Sharon & Bob Huxford
1202 7th Street
Covington, Indiana   47932

$9.95 plus 50¢ for postage
Copyright Bob & Sharon Huxford 1981
ISBN: 0-89145-168-4

TABLE OF CONTENTS

FOREWORD

"Outsells ALL leading competitors, three to one!!
Ovenproof, durable, resists cracking and chipping!
The MOST versatile line of dinnerware EVER produced! Dollar for dollar, the BEST buy around!"

Products come and go, and by and large 90% of the advertising our ears and eyes are bombarded with today is strictly "hype"—10% might qualify for something you could depend on. And we're **all** weary of hearing false claims, misleading statements, and promises that are obviously impossible to keep. You know the ones—"grow a full head of hair in just 14 days . . .loose up to 10 lbs. the first week . . .you'll never have to (a) spray for bugs, (b) wax your floor, or (c) replace your oil filter . . .ever again!"

But had the Homer Laughlin China Co. been as bold in 1936 as advertisers are today, it is obvious to us who love Fiesta—or any of their other lovely wares—that any claim would have been 100%! And had they been able to foresee the future and their unprecedented success, they might have added more, all very truthful:

"Unlimited appeal! Sought by thousands—all ages, every occupation! A source of enjoyment and satisfaction to collectors everywhere . . .and a sound investment!"

For it's all of that and more. It's a trip into nostalgia, yet as fresh as each new day! Many of us will find it difficult to imagine our lives as they would have been without it. For each lovely piece in our collections has a story to tell all its own . . .of pleasant outings, of new friendships—this one a gift, that one so elusive! Its gay, vibrant colors seem somehow reflected in our lives.

We hear from new collectors almost daily, and those who began with us several years ago are branching out and becoming more diversified. Harlequin accessories are more rare than their Fiesta counterparts, and veteran collectors love the challenge! Medium green has become **the** color, and there is a growing interest in the Mexican decaled lines. These and other new trends, new discoveries, and new values are covered in this fourth chapter of the story of Fiesta, and whether or not this is the conclusion remains to be seen. We hope you will continue to let us hear of "new finds"; sharing them with our readers has been for us a real pleasure.

ABOUT THE AUTHORS

From a long-time interest in collecting, the Huxfords have expanded their hobby to include research and writing, and both agree they find this field to be the most exciting and rewarding. Their first book, **THE STORY OF FIESTA** was published in 1974, and is now in its fourth edition. They have written several other books dealing with the Ohio potteries...**THE COLLECTORS ENCYCLOPEDIA OF ROSEVILLE POTTERY** and **THE COLLECTORS CATALOGUE OF EARLY ROSEVILLE** were published in 1976; new releases in 1978 included **THE COLLECTORS ENCYCLOPEDIA OF MC COY POTTERY, THE COLLECTORS ENCYCLOPEDIA OF BRUSH-MC COY POTTERY,** and **THE COLLECTORS CATALOGUE OF BRUSH-MC COY POTTERY. THE COLLECTORS ENCYCLOPEDIA OF WELLER POTTERY** was published in 1979, and in 1980 they wrote **THE COLLECTORS ENCYCLOPEDIA OF ROSEVILLE POTTERY, VOLUME II.**

ACKNOWLEDGEMENTS

For this our fourth edition, we found it necessary to rely more on our fellow collectors for help than ever before. Because the new items we wanted to show you came from collections all over the country, it was impossible to 'pack up' our own photographer and travel nationwide! Instead, for the first time we had to ask each donor to shoulder the responsibility of having his own items photographed—and felt it a real imposition to do so! But everyone responded with enthusiasm and promptly sent the photos we requested! And in order to provide you with as accurate a value guide as we possibly could, we contacted many dealers in various parts of the country and asked them to send us an average evaluation from their area. To all of you who sent photos or helped with pricing we send our sincere thanks:

Chester Sturm
J. W. Pons
Mrs. Donald Merryman
Mrs. Vera Barlow
Nancy Nowak and
    Ed McKenney

Florence and Lyle Ohlendorf
James E.Wolfe
Mrs. James Rice
Debbie and Frank Merritt
Ted Haun

We appreciate every one of you! But there are two people who we want to acknowledge with a very special "Thank you" . . .

Lucille and Austin Wilson

The Wilsons boxed up more than 150 pieces from their collection, located a photographer, arranged the set-ups and catalogued each piece. Our requests bordered on harrassment, but they remained always kind and helpful.

Thanks again to Rev. Leslie Wolfe and his wife Marjorie—our collaborators and long-time friends . . . and we will always appreciate the cooperation of Mr. Ed Carson, representative of the Homer Laughlin China Company for the interest he has shown in our efforts, and his invaluable assistance. To our readers, fellow collectors, and friends, "Thank you" . . .it's been a joy!

God Bless You All.

THE LAUGHLIN POTTERY STORY

The Laughlin Pottery was formed in 1871 on the River Road in East Liverpool, Ohio — the result of a partnership between Homer Laughlin and his brother, Shakespear Laughlin. The pottery was equipped with two periodic kilns and was among the first in the country to produce whitewares. Sixty employees produced approximately 500 dozen pieces of dinnerware per day. The superior quality of their pottery won for them the highest award at the Centennial Exposition in Philadelphia in 1876.

In 1879, Shakespear Laughlin left the pottery, and, for the next 10 years, Homer Laughlin carried on the business alone. William Edwin Wells joined him in 1889 and, at the end of 1896, the firm incorporated. Shortly thereafter, Laughlin sold his interests to Wells and a Pittsburgh group headed by Marcus Aaron.

Under the new management, Mr. Aaron became President, with Mr. Wells acting in the capacity of Secretary-Treasurer and General Manager.

As their business grew and sales increased, the small River Road plant was abandoned and the company moved its location to Laughlin Station, three miles east of East Liverpool. Two large new plants were constructed and a third purchased from another company. By 1903, all were ready for production. A fourth plant was built in 1906 at the Newell, West Virginia site, and began operation in 1907. In 1913, with business still increasing, Plant 5 was added.

The first revolutionary innovation in the pottery industry was the continuous tunnel kiln. In contrast to the old batch-type, or periodic kilns which were inefficient from a standpoint of both fuel and time, the continuous tunnel kiln provided a giant step toward modern day mass production. Plant 6, built in 1923, was equipped with this new type kiln and proved so successful that two more such plants were added, Plant 7, in 1927, and Plant 8, in 1929. The old kilns in Plants 4 and 5 were replaced in 1926 and 1934 respectively.

In 1929 the old East Liverpool factories were closed, leaving the entire operation at the Newell, West Virginia site.

At the height of their production the company grew to a giant concern which employed 2,500 people, produced thirty thousand dozen pieces of dinnerware per day, and utilized 1,500,000 square feet of production area. In contrast to the early wares, painstakingly hand-fashioned in the traditional methods, the style of ware reflected the improved mass production techniques which had of necessity been utilized in later years. The old-fashioned dipping tubs gave way to the use of high-speed conveyor belts and spray glazing, and mechanical jiggering machines replaced for the most part the older methods of man powered molding machines.

In 1930, W. E. Wells retired from the business after more than 40 years of brilliant leadership, having guided the development and expansion of the company from its humble beginning on the Ohio river to a position of unquestioned leadership in its field. He was succeeded by his son, Joseph Mahan Wells. Mr. Aaron became Chairman of the Board, and his son, M. L. Aaron, succeeded him as President. Under their leadership, in addition to the successful wares already in production, many new developments made possible the production of a wide variety of utilitarian wares including the oven-to-table ware, Oven Serve and Kitchen Kraft. Later, the creation of the beautiful colored glazes which have become almost synonymous with Homer Laughlin, resulted in the production of the colored dinnerware lines which have captured the attention of many collectors today — Fiesta, Harlequin, and Riviera.

On January 1, 1960, Joseph M. Wells became Chairman of the Board, and his son Joseph M. Wells, Jr. followed him in the capacity of Executive Vice-President.

Today, Homer Laughlin employs 1,600 workers, producing approximately 60 million pieces of dinnerware per year.

VACATIONING IN THE MORGUE???
(we loved it!)

Have you ever awakened from your dreams, been able to close your eyes once again, concentrate very hard, and remember some heretofore completely unheard of piece of Fiesta . . . or Harlequin . . . or Riviera? I remember some fantastic tall stemmed mugs that distinctly and to my absolute joy were marked "Genuine Fiesta" when I turned them up to check!! How disappointing to discover it was only a dream!

Last fall, on a return trip to HLC, we were allowed an experience that was to us as exciting as having our dreams come true. We were granted permission to explore the "morgue"! What a name to call such a delightful place! Better than any junk store . . . more "goodies" than anyone could dream of!

We dug in shelves and boxes to our hearts' content. We photographed and catalogued all the things we found. Jane, a very sweet lady in engineering, kept all the Fiesta we dug out and cleaned up together in boxes, in hopes that someday a display might be arranged for future visitors to enjoy.

There were familiar Fiesta, Harlequin and Riviera there, to be sure; but what captured our attention were the many experimental pieces. The very first beautiful and unfamiliar piece of Fiesta we saw was an ivory individual tea pot with a stick handle, 6" tall. It had a globular shape, and its lid was interchangeable with the demitasse coffee pot. Although it was never produced for the market, at least one has been found in a shop in Newell, West Virginia, by a very lucky collector!

We learned that the designer, Fredrick Rhead, modeled many pieces which were never marketed, due to the onset of the war scare . . . when lines already in production were cut back.

10

There was a relish plate with five compartments, arranged just like your Fiesta relish tray, but molded in one piece. It was in navy and was decorated with a band of rings . . . had the look of Fiesta, but may not have even been an HLC product. We were astounded to learn the extent at which potteries "borrowed" designs and patterns from each other . . . evidently very goodnaturedly.

Another piece we found was an ivory 6″ vase which might best be described as looking like the pouring end of two disk juice pitchers, back to back, with the ice lips removed! The body was a round upright disk, and the band of rings design was a complete circle, slightly indented into the front and back sides.

There was a yellow piece, 5″ across, flat and very shallow, with a narrow flat rim. Although most of the experimental pieces were marked with only code numbers, this one carried the familiar "Fiesta" cast-indented mark.

Stacked in a corner were several sections of a large relish designed by Rhead. Four trays with three compartments, each was styled with the intent of being used on a large oval wooden base. Although never released, one of these sections is shown on page 79.

A piece that looked very familiar to us, except for its size (it was 6½″ tall) was done in yellow, and scaled to perfection to the lines of the syrup bottom.

And the experimental colors were fantastic! There was a rich burgundy wine cream soup, and a relish tray done in the Wells Matt Glaze, which had the effect of iron rust. Plates were in dark brown with an orange splattered effect, a blue plum, a dark russet tone, a deep, deep gold, and our favorite of all — black with four chromium bands, which must have been 35 years ahead of its time.

Some familiar Kitchen Kraft items had been glazed in pastels — pink, light blue, pale yellow and mint green — and the mark stamped on the bottom of some identified the line as "Chromatics".

From a box in a corner, came the metal holder for the pie plate — the first we had seen. These, the metal holders for the Kitchen Kraft casseroles and the one for the oval Kitchen Kraft platter, were shipped to HLC and distributed from the factory with these pieces. However, not all were sold with holders. We also found the underplates for the casseroles. These were simply a flat plate with a rim, seemingly of a lighter weight than usual. We wondered if perhaps they were from another line and simply dipped in the Fiesta Kitchen Kraft colors.

Several small nut dishes with a basketweave design were stacked on a shelf, next to a larger one . . . identical except for the addition of some flowers inside the bowl. We learned that the smaller version was from the Harlequin line, and had been copied from the larger, which was a Japanese import. There was a matching bowl (but this had been only experimental, and had not been marketed), and an ash tray with the basketweave design; it also belonged to the Harlequin line.

There were two styles of experimental candlesticks in Harlequin. One pair was large and flat, 5½″ wide and 2¼″ tall in the center. The other pair were shaped like half of an inverted cone, 4¼″ across the bottom and 3″ tall. Both styles were lovely, but not quite as nice as our regular candleholders. The only other unusual Harlequin piece was a 5″ fruit, shaped almost like the small Fiesta fruit dish. There were some novel experimental colors . . . chocolate brown, deep golden tan, a pale bisque beige, lavender, vanilla, and a beautiful plate, cup and saucer in a high gloss black!

We found three sizes in Riviera butters, 9″, 6½″, and 7½″. The latter, although just the right size for a quarter-lb. stick of today's butter, was never marketed. Also strictly experimental — and what a shame — was a large footed console bowl, 15″ × 8½″ and a pair of tall, 6″ candleholders. These really were beautiful. Of all the discoveries we made, they held the most appeal to us!

Have you ever wondered about the six sections around the Riviera shakers? They were originally designed to go with the Tango line, but as the shape was compatible, they were also used with Riviera. Tango was a colored dinnerware line made for promotion through Newberry's. Colors were green, yellow, burgundy, and blue; there may have been others. The gauge was similar to Harlequin, the design was a classic Colonial style; but, for some reason, it was not a good seller.

We so thoroughly enjoyed our day in the morgue, and we felt that we would like to share some of its contents with all our readers. Although most of the beautiful pieces we saw will never be available to the collector, like the little individual tea pot, there may be a few that somehow found their way to the outside. When our day was over, we felt reluctant to close that door, with its double lock, and to have to leave behind it those lovely pieces. They were truly "stuff that dreams are made of"!

. . . that RADIOACTIVE RED!

Exactly when the first rumors began circulating . . . hinting that the red Fiesta could be "hazardous" to your health, is uncertain. In most probability, it was around the time that Fiesta red was reintroduced, after the war . . . and was no doubt due to the publicity given to uranium and radio-activity during the war years. Clearly another case where "a *little* learning can be a dangerous thing".

In any case, this worry must have remained to trouble the minds of some folks for several years. Even today the subject comes up occasionally and remains a little controversial, even though most folks in this troubled age of ozone worries, no-phosphates, or cyclamates, cholesterol-free diets, and constant reminders that "Cigarettes are hazardous to your health" don't really seem too upset by it any more.

The following letter appeared in the *Palm Beach Post Times,* in February, 1963. It was written "tongue-in-cheek" by a man who had evidently reached the limit of his patience. HLC sent it to us from their files; it has to be a classic. Here it is . . .

Editor:

After reading about the radioactive dishes in your paper I am greatly concerned that I may be in danger, as I had a plate with a design in burnt orange, or maybe it was lemon.

This plate was left to me by my great grandmother, and I noticed that whenever she ate anything from it her ears would light up so we all had to wear dark glasses when dining at her house.

I first became suspicious of this dish when putting out food for my dog on it I noticed the dog's nose became as red as Rudolph's and one day a seagull fed from it and all his feathers fell off; then one night when the weather was raw I placed it at the foot of my bed and my toenails turned black.

Using it as a pot cover while cooking eel stew, the pot cracked; and reading the letters in your paper last week have concluded I am not the only person having a cracked pot in the house, so perhaps some of your other readers used a plate for a cover.

I finally threw this plate overboard at a turn in the channel, now a buoy is no longer needed there, as bubbles and steam mark this shoal.

Will you please ask your Doctor or someone if they think this plate was radioactive, and if so am I in any danger, and if so from what?

(Name Withheld)

In case the question ever arises in your presence, the following information will provide you with an intelligent answer. This data was measured at Purdue University in the Bionucleonics Department by Dr. Paul L. Ziemer, and Dr. Geraldine Deputy, who herself is an avid Fiesta collector. Here are the results of their study:

The penetrating radiation from the depleted uranium oxide used in the manufacturing of the glaze for the "red" Fiestaware was measured with a standard laboratory Geiger Counter. All measurements are tabularized in units of milliroentgens per hour (mR/hr).

ITEM	SURFACE CONTACT	4" ABOVE SURFACE	ALONG RIM
13" Chop Plate	0.8	0.35	0.1
9" Plate	0.5	1.5	0.07
Fruit Bowl	1.5	0.5	0.1
Relish Tray Wedge	0.8	0.2	0.02
Cup	1.3	0.2	0.03

In order to compare the above values to familiar quantities of radiation we calculated the exposure of a person holding a 13" chop plate strapped to his chest for 24 hours. This gives 20 milliroentgens per day. Safe levels for humans working with radiation is 100 milliroentgens per week for a 5 day week or 20 milliroentgens per day as background radiation.

Some other measurements of interest for comparison purposes are:

ITEM	RADIATION
Radium Dial on a Watch	20 mR/hr
Chest X-Ray	44mR per film
Dental X-Ray	910 mR per film
Fatal Dose	400,000 mR over whole body

So you see — unless you've noticed your grandmother's nose glowing — we're all quite safe!

One other *tiny* worry to put to rest . . . some have mentioned it . . . there is no danger from the fired-on glazes which are safe as opposed to a shellac-type color which could mix with acid from certain foods, and result in lead poisoning.

Wouldn't it be good to get back to the days when worries were simple and uncomplicated . . . and everybody cooked with lard and had never heard of cholesterol . . . and air pollution was just something to be washed off white enameled woodwork at spring cleaning time . . . and gas was 25¢ a gallon . . .

Post Script: As recently as May, 1977, on an Eastern television station, an announcement was made concerning the pros and cons of the safety of colored glazed dinnerware. Fiesta was mentioned by name. We contacted the Department of Health, Education and Welfare, FDA, in Chicago, Illinois. This in part is their position, and is supported by HLC:

"The presence of lead, cadium and other toxic metal in glaze or decal is not in itself a hazard. It becomes a problem only when a glaze or decal that has not been properly formulated, applied or fired, contains dangerous metals which can be released by high acid foods such as fruit juices, some soft drinks, wines, cider, vinegar and vinegar containing foods, sauerkraut, and tomato products" . . .

HLC passed the rigorous federal tests with flying colors! In fact, the only examples of earthenware posing a threat to consumers were imported, and hobbyists were warned to use extreme caution in glazing hand thrown ceramics.

The FDA report continues:

"be on the safe side by not storing foods or beverages in such containers for prolonged periods of time, such as overnight. Daily use of the dinnerware for serving food *does not* pose a hazard. If the glaze or decal is properly formulated, properly applied, and properly fired, there is no hazard."

. . . R. I. P.

17

A WORD TO THE WISE . . . . .

Haven't we all had the experience of finding a likely looking piece of pottery . . . we ponder and study, turn it over and over, flip the rim to make it ring, compare color and glaze, weight and thickness . . . and still be at a complete loss???

Probably the most important lesson to be learned, especially in this area of collecting, is that no matter how good a piece looks, be extremely suspicious! Styles, designs, decorations, and even glazes were flagrantly copied from one pottery by another. Whole lines were stolen from pottery dumps!

By now, many of you have been collecting the various colored dinnerware lines of HLC for seven years or so . . . some perhaps even longer. We have become much more aware of the similar wares produced by Knowles; Taylor, Smith & Taylor; Bauer and many others; and we are better educated and equipped to determine which of the many "lookalike" wares are indeed properly bred and truly deserving of a home in our exclusively Homer Laughlin collections.

But to the newer collectors, this can be very confusing, to say the least! Once we become familiar with the wonderful glazes used for Fiesta and Harlequin, strange pieces in exactly those colors seem to "come out of the woodwork"—coyly enticing—and in our enthusiasm it is sometimes difficult to place them in their proper perspective! Many manufacturers produced numerous lines of these gaily colored wares and it is impossible in most cases to determine the origin of any piece by the color or quality of the glaze alone. For instance, the Bauer California Pottery produced their Ring pattern in some of the same colors as Fiesta—Taylor, Smith and Taylor made Vistosa, with its pastry crimped rims and holloware handles each daintily accented with a tiny blossom, in Fiesta-like red, cobalt blue, yellow and light green! Caliente's streamlined styling featured holloware whose bases were designed with four petal-like feet, and its colors were also similar—Tangerine, yellow, blue and green. There was Yorktown by Knowles, and a line by Stangl—at least three by the Paden City Pottery—not to mention numerous others, (even one from Japan) and all were aimed at catching the "magic ring"—at becoming the favorite of the American people who had fallen in love with color!

Nor was the "band of rings" decoration exclusive with HLC. Bauer's Modern (1935) is very similar to Fiesta. Yorktown by Knowles, Hamilton Ross's Harlequin look-alike . . .all were geared to the Deco movement—clean fluid geometry in precision arrangements of lines and angles.

So that you may easily recognize the Homer Laughlin wares, study the shapes in the color plates. This is the key. We still occasionally hear of those who refuse to buy unmarked ware. This practice is unnecessary. Although there are many imitations, none of these lines have ever been copied so precisely that anyone who makes an effort to become familiar with their appearance cannot distinguish them from even their closest look-alike.

There are several items shown in the color section that are especially confusing to new collectors—others continue to surface. We once saw a turquoise casserole that looked exactly like the Fiesta casserole, except this one had no foot. It was marked "Tricolator Products, U.S.A." It seemed logical to assume that these were manufactured at HLC for Tricolator Products. But a company official cleared up the mystery with this statement:

"It is unthinkable that with the popularity of Fiesta, that we would sell Fiesta items under another company's name." Another imitation! There are bulb-type candleholders very similar to Fiesta's . . .salt and pepper shakers of many types—one curious set consisted of what appeared to be a genuine Fiesta salt shaker perched atop a little raised platform with handles, which was actually the pepper! (HLC had never heard of it!)

Then of course, there are always "Fiesta butter dish" stories from time to time. Here is HLC's report:

> "If you do find the butter in Fiesta, it will necessarily be a copy, because this certainly was one of the items that was never produced in this line based upon all records available and the memories of those people involved in designing, manufacturing, and shipping Fiesta over the years."

Although such reports have become infrequent, there may even yet be an undiscovered item or two . . . perhaps a one-of-a-kind whimsy created by an inventive craftsman. These things have always been. Even through the years of mass production, that desire innate in every living person to make something with his own hands, using his own ideas is strong in his breast. The temptation to create in an environment where all the necessary materials and equipment are available would be too much for the craftsman so inclined to put from his mind! In the color section you will see several lamps whose sections are fashioned from comport stems, casserole bowls, nappies, and fruit dishes. A company spokesman recalls that some of their employees fashioned lamps for themselves from carafe bottoms. Others used tall vases.

One last item that may be confusing some of you . . . it certainly did us . . . is the pie plate with an exact duplication of the Harlequin rings. We have seen one in green, and the color is a perfect match. This is a classic example. HLC says it is not Harlequin, nor did they produce it. So be cautious . . . we would welcome your inquiries if you have questions about identification. If there are new discoveries—and there may yet be—we will do our best to keep our fellow collectors informed and up to date!

THE STORY OF FIESTA

In January of 1936, Homer Laughlin introduced a sensational new line of dinnerware at the Pottery and Glass Show in Pittsburgh. It was "Fiesta" . . . and it instantly captured the imagination of the trade — a forecast of the success it was to achieve with housewives of America.

Fiesta was designed by Fredrick Rhead, an English Stoke-on-Trent potter, who was employed under the direction of M. L. Aaron, President, and J. M. Wells, Secretary and General Manager. His design was modeled by Arthur Kraft and Bill Bersford. The distinctive glazes were developed by Dr. A. V. Blenininger in association with H. W. Thiemecke.

A talc body was introduced for the first time, making Fiesta entirely different in body materials and glazes. This made it necessary to confine its production to the Number 4 plant, in Newell, West Virginia. This plant soon led all others in output and production, due to Fiesta's unprecedented popularity. Opinion in the beginning was that certain sections of the country would not like the colorful ware and the unusual shapes. However, sales were ever-increasing on a nationwide basis!

This popularity was the result of much planning, market analysis, creative development, and a fundamentally sound and well-organized styling program. Rather than present to the everyday housewife a modernistic interpretation of a formal table service which might have been received with some reservation, HLC offered a more casual line with a well-planned series of accessories whose style was compatible with any decor and whose vivid colors could add bright spots of emphasis. Services of all types could be chosen and assembled at the whim of the housewife, and the simple style could be used compatibly with other wares already in her cabinets.

In an article by Fredrick Rhead, taken from the "Crockery and

Glass Journal" for June, 1937, these steps toward Fiesta's development were noted:

First, from oral descriptions and data concerning most generally used table articles, a chart of tentative sketches in various appealing colors was made. As the final ideas were formulated, they were modified and adjusted until development was completed.

Secondly, the technical department made an intensive study of materials, compositions, and firing temperatures. During this time models and shapes were being studied. The result was to be a streamline shape, but not so obvious as to detract from the texture and color of the ware. It was to have no relief ornamentation, and was to be pleasantly curving and convex, rather than concave or angular. Color was to be the chief decorative note, but to avoid being too severe, the concentric band of rings were to be added at the edges.

Since the early thirties, there had been a very definite trend in merchandising toward promoting "color". Automobiles, household appliances and furnishings, ladies' apparel . . . all took on vivid hues. The following is an excerpt from Rhead's article: (although he relates the ivory glaze being chosen as the fifth color, it was not an original color, but was added later on in 1936).

"The final selection of five colors was a more difficult job because we had developed hundreds of tone values and hues and there were scores which were difficult to reject. Then, there were textures ranging from dull mattes to highly reflecting surfaces. We tackled the texture problem first. (Incidentally, we had made fair sized skeletons in each of the desirable glazes in order to be better able to arrive at the final selection.)

We eliminated the dull mattes and the more highly reflecting glazes. First, because in mass production practice, undue variation would result in unpleasant effects. The dull surfaces are not easy to clean and the too highly reflecting surfaces show "curtains" or variations in thickness of application. We decided upon a semi-reflecting surface of about the texture of a billiard ball. The surface was soft and pleasant to the touch and in average light there were no disturbing reflections to detract from the color and shape.

We had one lead with regard to color. There seemed to be a trade preference for a brilliant orange red. With this color as a key note and with the knowledge that we were to have five colors, the problem resolved to one where the remainder would "tune in" or form appropriate contrasts.

The obvious reaction to red, we thought, would be toward a fairly deep blue. We had blues ranging from pale turquoises to deep violet blues. The tests were made by arranging a table for four people and, as the plate is an important item in the set, we placed four plates on various colored cloths and then arranged the different blues around the table. It seemed that the deeper blues reacted better than the lighter tones and also blues which were slightly violet or purple. We also found that we had to do considerable switching before we could decide upon the right red. Some were too harsh and deep, others too yellow.

With the red and blue apparently settled, we decided that a green must be one of the five colors. We speedily discovered that the correct balance between the blue and the red was a green possessing a minimum of blue. We had to hit halfway between the red and the blue. We had some lovely subtle greens when they were not placed in juxtaposition with the other two colors, but they would not play in combination.

The next obvious color was yellow and this had to be toned halfway between the red and the green. Only the most

*brilliant yellow we could make would talk in company with
the other three.*

*The fifth color was the hardest nut to crack. Black was
too heavy, although this may have been used if we could
have had six or more colors. We had no browns, purples or
grays which would tune in. We eliminated all except two
colors: a rich turquoise and a lovely color we called rose
ebony. But there seemed too much color when any fifth was
introduced in any table arrangement. The quartette seemed
to demand a quieting influence, so we tried an ivory vellum
textured glaze which seemed to fit halfway between the yellow and the regular semi-vitreous wares and which cliqued
when placed against any one of the four colors selected. It
took a little time to sell the ivory to our sales organization,
but when they saw the table arrangements they accepted the
idea."*

In the same publication, a month earlier, Rhead had offered this
evaluation of the popularity of the various colors with the public:

*"When this ware first appeared on the market, we
attempted to estimate the preference for one color in comparison with the others. As you know, we make five colors
. . . Because the red was the most expensive color, we
thought this might affect the demand. And also, because
green had previously been a most popular color, some
guessed that this would outsell the others. However, to date,
the first four colors are running neck and neck with less
than one percent difference between them. This is a
remarkable result and amply bears out . . . that the "lay-
man" prefers to mix his colors."*

The original assortment presented in the four colors — green,
blue, yellow, and red, consisted of 54 items:

Flower vase, 10"; Coffee pot, regular; Tea pot, large; Tea Pot, medium; Coffee pot, A.D.; Carafe; Ice Pitcher; Jug, 2 pints; Covered sugar; Creamer; Bud vase; Chop plate, 15″; Chop plate, 13″; Compartment plate, 10½″; Plate, 10″; Plate, 9″; Plate, 7″; Plate, 6″; Tea cups and saucers; Coffee cups and saucers, A.D.; Footed salad bowl; Nested bowls, 11½″ to 5″; Covered casserole; Cream soup cup; Covered onion soup; Relish tray; Comport, 12″; Nappy, 9½″; Nappy, 8½″; Deep plate, 8″; Dessert, 6″; Fruit, 5″; Ash tray; Sweets comport; Candleholders, tripod; Candleholders, bulb type; Salt and pepper shakers; Marmalade; Mustard; Egg cups; Tumbler; Tom & Jerry mugs; Utility tray.

Adding further to the selling possibilities of Fiesta, in June, 1936, the company offered their "Harmony" dinnerware sets. These combined their Nautalis line decorated with a colorful decal pattern, accented and augmented with the Fiesta color selected for that particular set. N-258 featured yellow Fiesta, accenting Nautalis in white decorated with a harmonizing floral decal at the rim. N-259 used green Fiesta to complement a slender spray of pine cones. Red Fiesta, in N-260, was shown together with the Nautalis decorated with lines and leaves in an Art Deco flavor; and Blue (N-261) went well with the white Nautalis with an off-center flower-filled basket decal. These sets were composed of 76 pieces in this combination:

NAUTALIS SHAPE	FIESTA
8 7″ plates	8 10″ plates
8 4″ plates	8 7″ plates
8 tea cups and saucers	8 6″ plates
8 4″ fruits	1 15″ chop plate
1 10″ baker	1 12″ comport
1 7″ nappy	2 bulb candlesticks
	1 salt and pepper
	1 sugar and creamer

Retail price for such a set was around $20.00; with Fiesta red increasing the total cost by about $3.50. This offered a complete service for 8 and extra pieces that allowed for buffet and party service for as many more of the contrasting items.

For some time during the earlier years of production, beautifully accessorized "Fiesta Ensembles" were assembled—you will see a picture of a display ad showing such a set in the color plates. It contains 109 pieces, only 40 of which are Fiesta:

8 9" plates
8 6" plates
8 tea cups and saucers
8 5" fruits

Accessories include:

24 pc. glassware set, with Mexican decal, 8 each 10 oz., 8 oz., and 6 oz. tumblers
8 color coordinated swizzle sticks
8 glass ashtrays
Service for 8, flatware with color coordinated plastic handles
1 serving bowl in red Riviera
1 15½" red Riviera platter
1 sugar and creamer in green Riviera

Included with this was a promotional poster advertising this set for the sum of $14.95 . . . enough to dazzle the heart of any housewife, whether she were a bride or a grandmother!

By way of correction, we were in error concerning the origin of these sets. Our information came from more than one source, and after so many, many years had elapsed, it is quite understandable that sometimes memories failed! Here, with our apologies, is HLC's statement which certainly clears up the issue:

"Silverware and glassware sold in Fiesta ensembles were manufactured by other companies and merely shipped here to our plant and reshipped with the Fiesta and other items included in the ensemble. Records fail to identify the company that may have manufactured these complimentary accessories."

Several unusual items have recently been discovered, and we feel must be attributed to the very early years of production before the war scare caused a cut-back. Records were not well kept, especially during these very early years. An example of this are the lids for the nested bowls, recently verified from an illustration in an old trade paper. At least four sizes of these lids have been located, made to fit the # 1 through # 4 nested bowls.

Early in 1938, a sixth color — turquoise — was chosen to be added to the existing five.

By July 1, 1938, the covered onion soup and the small compartment plate had been dropped from production and the stick handled creamer had been restyled with a ring handle by 1941. There is a 5″ fruit listed on the 1937 list, however by 1939 the listing shows a 5½″ and a 4¾″ fruit. Possibly the 5″ and the 5½″ are the same size fruit, with the so-called 5″ listed actual size in 1939 due to the addition of the 4¾″. In comparing actual measurements to listed measurements, we found variations of as much as ¾″. Assuming the smaller fruit to be the one added in 1939 would account for the scarcity of this item in red — since red was discontinued in 1943 and not made available again until 1959.

Three other items made their first appearance on the 1938 price lists — the 12″ platter, the sauceboat, and the disk water jug.

From 1939 through 1943 the company was involved in a promotional campaign designed to stimulate sales. This involved six special items, each originally offered for sale at 98¢ — the covered refrigerator jars, casserole and pie plate, handled chop plate, French casserole, individual sugar and creamer and tray, and a juice set consisting of a 30 ounce disk pitcher and six 5 ounce tumblers.

These items are not at all easy to find, except for the juice set, which must have been a popular item, since so many are seen yet today. This message was carried on an original flyer from HLC to their distributors.

"JUICE SET IN "FIESTA" . . . To help increase your

sales!" Homer Laughlin is offering an unusual value in the famous Fiesta ware . . . a colorful, 7-piece Juice Set, calculated to fill a real need in the summer refreshment field. The set consists of a 30-oz. disc jug in lovely Fiesta Yellow, and six 5-oz. tumblers, one each in the Fiesta blue, turquoise, red, green, yellow and ivory. Sets come packed one to a carton, and at the one dollar minimum retail price, are sure to create an upward surge in your sales curve. Dealers who take advantage of this Juice Set in Fiesta will find it a potent weapon in increasing sales of other Fiesta items. At a nominal price, customers who have not yet become acquainted with Fiesta, can own some of the ware which has made pottery history during the past few years. The result? They'll want to own more!

Very attractive "bait" that evidently landed many devotees! Although yellow was to have been the standard color for all juice pitchers, several have been found in red, one in grey, and one in light green. It is not, however, totally impossible to find one in some other color due to human error, or because of the whim of an employee with a particular color preference! In so large an operation, this must have occurred many times. We often wondered how the rose color was used for the juice tumblers, since it was not to become a regular Fiesta color for several years. A factory spokesman explained to us that, at this time, the rose glaze had been developed and was already a standard Harlequin color. Since it was available, it was used to add extra color contrast in the juice set. This may also be the reason that a few of the 4¾" fruits are found in medium green.

Occasionally, the juice set is found with a blue-grey pitcher, grey, ivory, and pale pink tumblers. These were dipped to go with a pastel line called Seranade . . . HLC's competition for TS&T's Lu Ray Pastels.

We mentioned in our first book that all of the French casseroles that we had seen were yellow. As with the juice pitchers, yellow was to have been the only color used, and we have never seen any other.

However, one in dark blue has been reported, and a friend has a lid in light green. Again, all individual sugars and creamers were to have been only yellow, and the trays dark blue. But a few red creamers have been found, and several trays in turquoise. Only recently, a sugar was reported in turquoise, and a tray in yellow.

In 1943 our government assumed control of uranium oxide, and as Fiesta red was manufactured from depleted uranium oxide, this color was dropped from production — "Fiesta Red went to war." Perhaps the fact that Fiesta red was always listed separately and priced proportionately higher than the other colors was due, in part, to the higher cost of raw material, plus the fact that the red items required strict control during firing and the losses that did occur had to be absorbed in the final costs.

The color assortment in 1944 included Turquoise, Green, Blue, Yellow, and Old Ivory. The 1944 price list no longer shows the tripod candleholders, nested bowls, or the 10″ and 12″ flower vases.

Although the colors are listed the same for the 1946 price list, the following pieces were no longer available: Bud vase, bulb type candleholders, carafe, 12″ comport, sweets comport, 8″ vase, 11½″ fruit bowl, ice pitcher, marmalade, mustard, 9½″ nappy, footed salad bowl, large tea pot, tumblers, and utility tray.

From 1946 through 1950 we have found no written information nor can the factory provide us with any. Perhaps, at some time during these four years, the color assortment was changed; we can't be sure. However, the October 1, 1951, price list does show these changes, and this may or may not have been the first year for them. Light Green, Navy Blue and Old Ivory were retired from active duty some time after the war was over — and their replacements were Forest Green, Rose, Chartreuse, and Grey, augmented by two old standards, Turquoise and Yellow.

If you have fallen into the habit of referring to these new colors as the "war colors", as we have, they might be more accurately dubbed

"Fifties' colors", since they and the listed assortment remained in production unchanged until 1959.

It is interesting to note, in comparing two 1956 price lists, one designated New Pacific coast retail, that prices were slightly higher on the West coast, probably due to transportation costs.

The big news in 1959 was, of course, the fact that Fiesta Red had finished her patriotic duty and was welcomed back home with much ado! The Atomic Energy Commission licensed The Homer Laughlin China Company to again buy the depleted uranium oxide and Fiesta Red, the most popular of all colors, returned to the market in May of 1959.

In addition to Red, Turquoise and Yellow, Medium Green was offered for the first time. The following items were no longer available:

15″ Chop plate; Coffee cups and saucers, A.D.; Coffee pots, regular; 10½″ compartment plates; Cream soup cups; Egg cups; 4¾″ fruit; 2 pint jug.

A new item makes a first appearance — the individual salad bowl. During the sixties, no changes were made either in the line or with the colors. Though retail prices had risen in 1965, by 1968 some items remained unchanged while others had actually dropped just a little.

In the latter months of 1969, in an effort to meet the needs of the modern housewife and to present a product that was better designed to be in keeping with modern day decor, Fiesta was restyled and only one of the original colors, Fiesta Red, always the favorite, continued in production.

As a footnote, we include a short chapter on Fiesta Ironstone, without which perhaps the story of Fiesta would not be complete. Due to its very contemporary flair and modern colors, however, we feel reluctant to include it in our story, except as a sequel. However, in the days to come — perhaps even now in the minds of some — Fiesta Ironstone will be as collectible as the old line.

IDENTIFICATION OF TRADEMARK, DESIGN AND COLOR

The original design, colors, and name are the registered property of the Homer Laughlin China Company, Patent No. 390-298 was filed on March 20, 1937, having been used by them since November 11, 1935. With only a few exceptions their distinctive trademark appears on every piece. These four seem to be the most common.

fiesta

HLC USA

H. L. C.

fiesta

MADE IN
U.S.A.

fiesta

MADE IN
U.S.A.

GENUINE

fiesta

H. L. Co.   USA
(Handstamped)

The indented trademark was the result of each item being marked in the mold while still in the clay state; the ink mark was put on by a handstamp, after the color was applied and before the final glaze was fired.

As many other manufacturers were following the trend to brightly colored dinnerware, the wide success and popularity of

Fiesta resulted in its being closely copied and produced at one time by another company. The Homer Laughlin Company quickly brought suit against their competitor and forced the imitation ware to be discontinued. Although there are those who contend that Fiesta was made by other manufacturers, "Genuine Fiesta" was the exclusive product of Homer Laughlin.

There are two other patterns which are at first sight easily confused with Fiesta. These are Harlequin and Riviera — not intended as imitations of Fiesta, but rather quite collectible in their own right. These were also made by Homer Laughlin, and we shall bring them to your attention again in another section.

There are some items in the Fiesta line which were never marked — juice glasses, demitasse cups, salt and peppers, and some of the Kitchen Kraft line. The tea cups were never to have been marked as a standard procedure, but a rare few have been found with the ink stamp. We have in our collection two covered onion soups; neither are marked. Never pass up a "goodie" such as these simply because they are unmarked — you may never own one! Sweets comports and ash trays may or may not be marked. As you become aware of the design and its familiar colors, these pieces will be easily identified as Fiesta.

Fiesta's design is very simple and therefore very versatile. The pattern consists of a band of concentric rings graduating in width, with those nearer the rim having the wider space between. The rings are repeated in the center motif on such pieces as plates, nappies, platters, desserts, etc. Handles are applied with slight ornamentation at the base. Flat pieces and bowls are round or oval, hollow-ware pieces are globular and many are styled with a short pedestal base, which also shows the band of rings.

But of course, it is Fiesta's vivid colors that first catch your attention. The wide array of color provides endless possibilities for matching color schemes and decor. Does Mediterranean best express your personality? Perhaps your choice will be Fiesta Red! Early American? Envision dark blue and grey with your pewter. A sunny breakfast nook becomes even more cheerful with a table set of bright yellow. Or perhaps your taste runs to simple elegance — shades of green and blue place settings, completely accessorized with Old Ivory.

But should you find you love all eleven colors, you'll surely enjoy collecting a place setting in every color — Fiesta Red, Rose, Old Ivory, Grey, Dark Blue, Light Green, Chartreuse, Dark Green, Turquoise, Yellow, and Medium Green. (Shown below, clockwise)

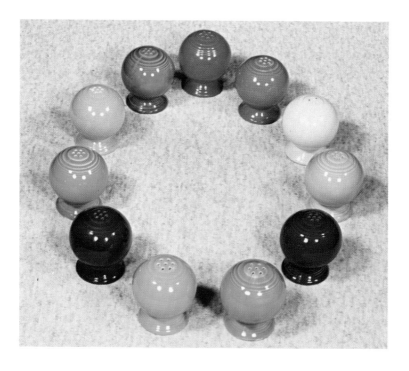

Question:
  When is it possible to "see red" and be happy at the same time???
Answer:
  (a) When it's Fiesta Red
  (b) When it's Harlequin Tangerine
  (e) When it's Riviera Red
  (d) *All* of the above!

NOW SHOWING . . . SPECIAL ADDED ATTRACTION
THE MEDIUM GREEN ENIGMA!!!

No, we're not talking about a rock group, but one of the most exciting of the Fiesta colors . . . and what makes it so exciting are those items that persistently "pop up" in medium green that we've never found listed on any company records as ever having been produced in that color! Not all of the pieces shown here are "enigmas" — but are never-the-less especially attractive to collectors in this color.

Top Row: 15″ and 13″ chop plates. Both sizes were in the original assortment. The larger size was discontinued around 1959, while the smaller continued in production until restyling. (We met a former restaurant owner, who told us that he used to send out steak dinners on Fiesta chop plates . . . only a few were returned for the deposit.)

Middle: 11⅝″ and 10½″ compartment plates. We never yet have found the larger plate listed and they seem to be a little hard to find; since no turquoise 11⅝″ has every been reported, we must assume these plates were in production for a short time before that color was added early in 1938. Not quite so scarce, the smaller size was in the original assortment. It's difficult to find in chartreuse, and was dropped from production before the advent of medium green.

Bottom: 10″ dinner plate, 9″ luncheon, 7″ bread and butter, 6″ dessert plate. Dinner plates in good condition are not as easy to come by as they were a few short years ago; some dealers report that any size in the 50's colors and medium green are becoming scarce and along with red, of course, are at the top rung of the price ladder. The number of rings on the back of a plate will vary—these identified the jiggerman and were a quality control device.

38

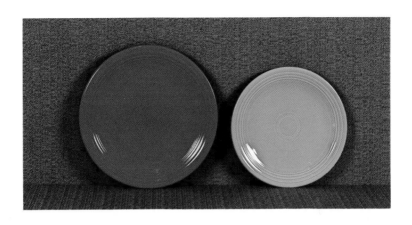

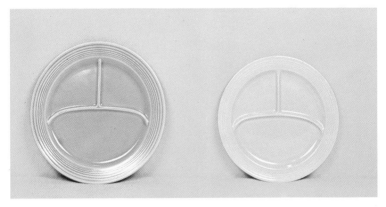

Top: Deep plate, 8″. This original item continued in production until restyling. Of course, it is found in all eleven colors, with red and the 50's colors most desirable.

Middle,
Left: Cream soup cup. These seem to be found without too much searching — watch for slight damage around the area of the handle or the foot. They were dropped by 1959, but a few have been found in medium green!

Center: Individual salad bowl, 7⅝″. This was a later piece, not being listed until 1959. Occasionally you may find one with no center rings, probably produced toward the period of transition into Ironstone. Although relatively rare in any color, red and medium green are found more often than turquoise and yellow. But due to its new found popularity, expect to pay premium price for one in medium green!

Middle,
Right: 6″ dessert bowl. This original piece was dropped around 1959, and medium green is hard to find.

Bottom: 4¾″ and 5½″ fruits. One of these was the original 5″ bowl, the other was added in 1939. We believe the smaller to be the 1939 bowl, due to the scarcity of this item in red. If so, then it would have been produced in red for 4 years only, before Fiesta Red went to war in 1943. Although not appearing on the 1959 price list with the new color assortment, a rare few have been found in medium green.

Top: Coffee pot, regular; tea cups and saucers. The coffee server was produced in all Fiesta colors, except med. green, since it was dropped just before 1959 . . . and those 50's colors are almost equal in value to red! Of course tea cups are much in demand. The cups with the inside rings are the older — notice, they also have a hand-turned foot.

A Colorado collector has reported a one-of-a-kind oddity—a saucer with a Fiesta die stamp! Ever seen one??

Middle: Egg cups. Although this is an original item and continued in production until just before 1959, they are not easily found. Yellow and turquoise are most common, and of the 50's colors, dark green and rose are most in demand . . . no medium green has been reported — yet! Ever wonder about the size? A lady explained this in a letter to us. She said that eggs used to be served poached, in such a large cup as this, so that one might have room to dunk his toast!

Lower
Right: Tom and Jerry mug. These little items are very popular and rising price tags reflect this fact. They were produced in all eleven colors; red ones are at a premium, and here's a surprise — ivory mugs are rare, and on the price scale seem to follow after red. Med. green is next, with the 50's colors led by dark green just behind.

Top: Disk pitcher, 10 oz. tumblers. Not original, but added to the line in 1939, this pitcher continued to be made until 1973. It seemed to be most scarce in chartreuse, followed by med. green, then dark green and rose. Perhaps least compatible with the bright colors of the tumblers, grey seems to be less popular. The tumblers were dropped in 1946, and you will find them only in the original six colors, with turquoise perhaps a little scarce. A friend has seen two ceramic type tiles in old ivory with decals depicting Fiesta. One shows a disk pitcher and a tumbler, while the other shows a coffee server and a tea cup and saucer. Wouldn't that be a "find"!!

Bottom: Sugar and creamer, regular, and stick handled creamer. The stick handled creamer was the original one, and was made in six original colors. It was restyled in 1941 with a ring handle.

Utility tray. An original item produced until 1946 in six original colors. These are in good demand; they're a little hard to find in red.

Salt and peppers. This was another original item that was made until the end. Aside from the larger Kitchen Kraft shakers, these are the only Fiesta shakers. You may find a good imitation, with shaker holes on the side . . . these are not Fiesta.

Top: Platter, 12". The first listing for this platter is 1939, although it then continued in production until restyling, when it was enlarged to 13".

9½" and 8½" nappies. Both sizes were original; however, the larger size was dropped in 1946. The 8½" carried through until restyling.

Yellow salad bowl, 9½". Although never found on company records, a trade paper once reproduced an old ad that offered this bowl complete with salad fork and server for 98¢! Although scarce in any color, yellow is standard, but at least one example each has been found in ivory, red and dark blue.

Center,

Left: Footed salad bowl. Rather hard to find, this bowl was dropped in 1946, and came only in red, dark blue, Old Ivory, yellow, turquoise, and lgt. green, with ivory and yellow being harder to find.

Bottom,

*Right:*11¾" fruit bowl. This was made for seven years only, between 1939 and 1945, in six original colors. They are rare in red . . .few in any color!

Top: Nested bowls — 11½″, 10″, 9″, 8″, 7″, 6″, 5″. These bowls, though original, were not found listed by 1944. They are numbered in sequence on the bottom. They are rather scarce, and very heavy! Stacked as a unit they weigh just under 20 lbs.!

#7 has now edged out #1 on the scarcity poll, with #2 and #3 being the most common. Lids are known to exist for #1 (5″) through #4 (8″), and there is an unconfirmed report on a #5 lid.

Center,
Left: Sauceboat. A beautifully designed Fiesta piece! Although not original, it was produced from '39 to the end in all colors.

This is a popular piece, and red and the colors of the 50's are increasingly hard to find.

Bottom,
Right: Covered casserole. Considering that production on this item was continuous from 1936, there are not many to be found. The design was completely changed at the restyling.

Hardest to find in med. green and dark green, these colors are often priced with the red!

49

Top: Relish tray. Five individual sections fit into the base on this very nice piece. You will find these in the six original colors only, since it was discontinued before 1946.

The base of the relish has often been mistaken for a pie plate; and even though those center sections certainly look like coasters, they were never produced or sold as such.

One particularly beautiful example of a Fiesta relish is considered by one collector-dealer-friend to be "the last piece I may ever part with"! Done in ivory, the base is filigreed in gold, and each individual section is decorated with a rose decal!

12″ comport. This piece is beautiful filled with fruit, or a candle and flowers. Discontinued before 1946, it was of course made only in red, dark blue, lgt. green, yellow, turquoise, and old ivory.

Bottom: Coffee Pot, A.D., cups and saucers. (After dinner). Although production stopped before 1944 on the pot, the demitasse cups and saucers continued until around 1951. The pot was made only in the original six colors; the cups in all but medium green. They are very rare in the rose, chartreuse, dark green, and grey; the pots are harder to find in red, turquoise, and ivory.

Imagine how beautiful the pot would be in a rich Burgandy wine! One collector has one, and sent us a photo to confirm the claim! It looked very much like an experimental glaze we saw in the morgue at HLC.

And a demitasse cup and saucer decorated by Royal China has been found with a 22 Kt. gold overall pattern of cherries and leaves, featuring an 18th Century garden scene—a suitor playing upon a flute to a properly demur lady with her fan, both elegantly attired in period costume.

Top: Carafe, 3 pt. This item was no longer listed on 1946 price lists. The top has a cork seal. Made only in six colors, its unique shape makes it a favorite among collectors.

Red is not only harder to find, but has "status" appeal; and ivory is also scarce.

Ice pitcher, 2 qt. Dropped before 1946, it was made in red, yellow, old ivory, lgt. green, dark blue and turquoise. Though its looks seem to suggest otherwise, it does not take a lid.

Ivory is the scarce one, although some dealers report low demand for this piece in any color but red.

Bottom: 2 pt. jug. This original item was produced until 1959 and was made in all colors but medium green.

It is most scarce in red, followed by dark green, rose and chartreuse.

Covered onion soup. Why would such a darling item have been the first to go? It wasn't even listed by 1939. As a result, they are very scarce, especially in turquoise. Red and ivory are also harder to find colors; with blue and yellow most common.

53

Top,

Clockwise: Ash tray, sweets comport, syrup pitcher, marmalade, and mustard. We found that the sweets comport, mustard and marmalade had been discontinued before 1946. (Spoons are not original). Mustards and marmalades are always in demand . . . red mustards are harder to find than red marmalades, and are usually very high! The ash trays were produced from '36-'73. The syrups rate high with collectors, red ones are relatively common, but again that "status" drives the price up! Ivory is the rare color!

A pair of shakers recently found at a rummage were made up of syrup bottoms fitted with metal tops, decorated with a painted design and "salt" and "pepper" lettering. Decades ago a tea company filled syrup bases with tea leaves, added a cork stopper and their label, and unwittingly contributed to the frustration of our time known to collectors who have only a bottom!

Bottom: Tea pot, large, 8 cups; tea pot, medium, 6 cups. The larger tea pot was an original item and was discontinued around 1945, being made, of course, in only the first six colors — red, blue, green, yellow, old ivory, and turquoise. The medium was original and continued to be produced until the line was discontinued.

Top: Vases, 10″, 8″, 12″ and Bud vase. The 10″ vase was the original size, although by May of '37 all three sizes were listed. By 1944 all had been discontinued but the 8″ vase, and, by 1946, it too was no longer available. All three sizes are very scarce, especially the 10″; the turquoise and ivory are harder-to-find colors. On the other hand, the bud vases, even though dropped before '46 are more readily available. All were produced in six older colors only.

A word of caution: We have noticed in some areas for dealers to price the bud vases in the range of the 8″ vase. This is a misconception. Don't be mislead by these high prices—refer to the price guide!

Bottom,
Left: Tripod Candleholders. A pair of these unusual candleholders would be a fine addition to any collection, but they are some of the rarer items in the line. Discontinued around '42 or '43, they were made only in the six original colors.

Bottom,
Right: Bulb type candleholders. Although these were made for only two years longer than the tripods, they are much easier to find. They are available in the same color assortment as the tripods.

These are four of six special promotional items offered by HLC from 1939-43. They were originally offered for sale at 98¢ and were part of a campaign designed to stimulate sales. The other two items included in this campaign were the covered refrigerator jars, and the casserole, which sold with the pie plate. You will see these in the Kitchen Kraft section.

Top: Handled chop plate. This is the 13″ chop plate, fitted with a metal spring handle, one of the few metal accessories shipped directly from HLC. (Very scarce with this handle.)

French casserole. Its unique styling makes this a popular item among collectors. Although not as rare as once thought, they're still quite scarce. Yellow was to have been the standard color, but one has been reported in dark blue, and a lid in light green.

Individual sugar, creamer and tray. This was described to us at the factory as being a yellow sugar and creamer on a dark blue tray, but occasionally you will find a red creamer, and once in awhile a turquoise tray. At least one sugar exists in turquoise, and a collector has reported a yellow tray.

Bottom: 30 oz. juice pitcher, 5 oz. tumblers. Of the six promotional items, this is the only one that is easy to find. 99% of the pitchers are yellow . . . red ones are rare! Light green has been reported, and a friend has one in grey which was offered in 1952 along with the juice tumblers in ''green (dark green), yellow and chartreuse''! You may find a juice tumbler in brown Amberstone—if you are very lucky! Although rose was not a standard color until the 50's it was borrowed from the Harlequin line for contrast as early as 1939.

59

The tiered tidbit trays were not made at HLC, but were drilled and assembled by some other concern. Nor were the metal holders for the marmalades, mustard, salt and peppers ever supplied by Homer Laughlin. The metal holders for the Kitchen Kraft casseroles (7½" shown), oval platters and pie plates were shipped from the factory as complete units, as were the metal handles for the chop plates.

A collector has sent us a photo of her Fiesta pin-up lamp! Although certainly not of HLC manufacture, it's metal parts were evidently fashioned years ago by a metal company who wisely took advantage of Fiesta's popularity. A 7¾" plate fits flush against the wall, and a metal tube that conceals the electric cord emerges at the bottom just above the "rings", gracefully curves downward and then straight up, through a cup and saucer . . . the cup holds the light fixture, and the shade decorated with a fruit decal covers the bulb.

The large wooden salad bowl sets on a base banded in Fiesta colors; on the base is a sticker that reads "G. H. Specialty Co., Fiestawood." On the following page you will see a large lazy Susan of the same manufacturer.

The pastel juice set, as well as several of the Kitchen Kraft items, were dipped to go with the Serenade line, HLC's answer to TS&T's Lu Ray Pastels. These are highly prized by many collectors.

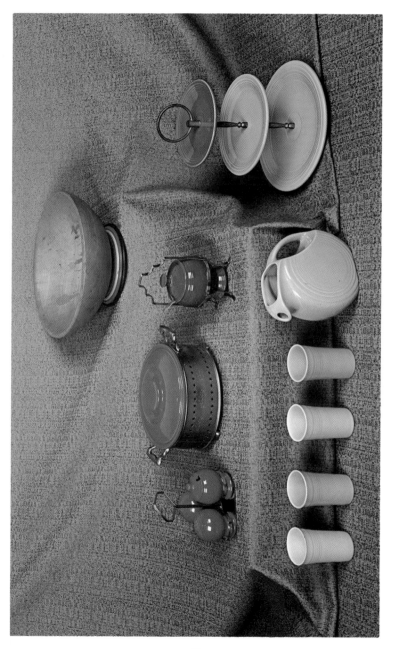

The nappy in the metal holder is the 9½". No information on this, but too many have been found in such a holder as to be coincidental.

The chrome frame for the cream soup converts it very nicely into a jam dish, and the large tea pot becomes a dripolator with the addition of the metal assembly (5½" high). These were original, although not from HLC. Nor was the wire frame for the juice set, but isn't it nice . . . very functional! Note the chartreuse juice tumbler, . . . very unusual! Look for one in dark green, these were a 1952 issue, part of a juice set with a grey pitcher and a yellow tumbler that completed the set.

This is the Sta-bright flatware, shown in each of four colors (yellow, red, green and black) that often accompanied Fiesta Ensembles. (See Page 26.)

The large (20" wide) lazy Susan is another Fiestawood piece by G. H. Specialty Co. Another tray very much like this one has indentions in the center area to hold a round jug-type pitcher and 8 tumblers.

These items are often marked with this ink stamp:

HOLLYWOOD
MERRY-GO-ROUND
Copyright 1936
G. H. SPECIALTY CO.
MILWAUKEE, WIS.

We have received photos of a holder for the Fiesta nappy in natural wood decorated with three bright hand painted red tomatoes, but with no mark to indicate the manufacturer.

Top: Metal holder for the ice pitcher and six 8 oz. tumblers. Attractive styling, completely complimentary to the spherical shape of the jug—yet totally practical and functional! Made by an enterprising metal company, not an HLC issue.

Bottom: Metal frame for the mustard and marmalade. Very nice Deco styling—sure to be on the want list of many collectors! The lovely relish tray is nestled in a gold filigreed base, and each piece is decorated with an underglaze floral decal. In the background, note the woven tablecloth with matching napkins displayed along the sides of the photo. Linens of this vintage in good condition provide a lovely setting for your Fiesta—or in fact, any of the Mexican patterned dinnerware lines shown later.

Top: The small teapot is decorated by hand with a fired on Pinecone spray. The Fiestawood in the center seems to be an hors d'oeuvre tray since the fish in the center is pierced to hold toothpicks. The border decoration is especially effective—stripes in festive colors punctuated by decals of a snoozing Mexican. On the right, a large KK covered jar is decorated with a decal of a patio scene, the table set with Fiesta-like dishes . . . the carafe and a shaker are especially familiar! The line is called Sun Porch!

Bottom
Left: One of a pair of boudoir lamps made from Fiesta syrup bottoms. A paper label on the back reads "Decorated by Dunhall". A lamp made from a Harlequin syrup and this identical base has also been found!

Bottom,
right: A Fiesta lamp! Actually, this is the fruits of someone's day-dreaming —isn't it attractive! Casserole bowls without their handles, stems from sweets comports, and a bowl for a base work well together to produce a striking lamp.

67

Top: Tom and Jerry set. This is the large salad bowl and the Tom & Jerry mugs, with gold bands and lettering. It's a beautiful set, and our friends to whom it belongs tell us they bought it for a "song" . . . stuck back under a table at an Antique Show!

Few complete sets have been located, mugs are more common than the bowls.

Middle: Two advertising pieces, in this case Tom & Jerrys advertising Pure Oil and O.K. Trucking. Both are very nice! The color of these mugs is white . . . not ivory!

Collectors have reported a variety of these, but one that captured our fancy is decorated with a caricature of Lucille Ball, signed "Love, Lucy", from the Desilu Studios. A report from our friends at the Fiesta Dishpatch reveals that The Jackson China Co. is producing a line of restaurant ware with a mug identical to HLC's Tom and Jerry. It is brown with a cream interior. The same Co. is also making a child's set consisting of a divided plate, a 6″ bowl, and the T & J mug in white decorated with a blue stenciled Donald Duck and friends.

Left: Homer Laughlin was quick to deny ever having had anything to do with these striped plates. Can you blame them! As you can see, they are not underglazed, and the stripes are usually very worn.

Top: The tall mugs in the top row are from a line of HLC hotel china, but note the Fiesta handle. The Sit 'n Sip sets are shown in the bottom row — the advertising mug with matching coaster — along with an original carton. The first mug on the second row is decorated with nursery characters.

Bottom: In addition to the turquoise and rose interiors shown, amberstone, turf green, and yellow have been found. The exterior glaze is white, not ivory! These were produced during the late 60's, into the early 70's. The bottom row are examples of a series decorated with decals of antique automobiles . . . six have been reported: 1924 Model "48" Buick, 1904 Model "B" Buick, 1936 Buick "Special", 1941 Buick Roadmaster, 1908 Model "10" Buick, 1916 Model "D" Buick. From 1964 through 1970 these Sit 'n Sip sets were issued for annual meetings of Buick Management, and their Salaried retirement club meetings. The collector that supplied this information also tells us that she has an ashtray dated 1963, Buick Management Meeting, Dec. 11-12. It is 8¾" round, raised in the center with six cigarette slots. Specialty items and advertising pieces are very popular with today's collector.

Top: This 15″ chop plate has been decorated by a smaller china company; both the decals and the gold trim are applied over the glaze. It's stamped "Vogue China". This Tom and Jerry set has lately been the center of much attention. Besides the more familiar T & J set on Fiesta shapes, HLC also made this set, and although perhaps not as sought after as the other, this one is very nice. Its lines are clean and simple; it would make a lovely addition to a Christmas buffet!

Bottom: Another Fiesta wood piece, this large tray measures 16½″. The ash tray is one we hunted for several years. On our first trip to HLC in 1972, we saw one on display, stamped in gold, as this one is, "1939, East Liverpool, Ohio, Rotary Club". We advertised for one in local papers while we were there to no avail, and had completely given up ever locating one when a lady from the East Liverpool area wrote, offering this one for trade. The metal lazy susan stand has a ball bearing section in between the disks that allows the top to rotate. The width of that flat rim fits between the rings under some 13″ and 15″ chop plates. This is another example of accessories made by companies other than HLC. The wood and metal handle nicely converts a Fiesta tumbler into a soda fountain mug . . . not of HLC manufacture.

73

Top: These commemorative pieces were made for the Lazarus Company, who issued them from 1938 through 1941 on their anniversary. Plates and tumblers may also be found.

Middle: This is the 15″ chop plate and a 7″ plate with a multi-floral decal in the center and the maroon rings around the rims. It is stamped "Fiesta" and is very rare.

The turkey decal is shown here on the 13″ chop plate. You may find it also on the 15″ size, as well as the dinner plate. This is an under-glaze decoration on commercial quality, according to HLC. These are very rare, also.

Bottom: The Homer Laughlin China Company issued a calendar plate for a number of years, using whatever blanks were available. In 1954 and 1955 they just happened to use Fiesta. The 9″ plate is the rare one . . . it may be found for either year; the 1954 plate has been found in ivory only, the '55 in green, yellow and ivory.

Top: This beautiful place setting of decaled Fiesta is part of a complete service. A lovely lady who loves Fiesta loaned it to us to show you. She is needing only a few pieces to replace some that are damaged. Please let us know if you have any. Another lucky collector sent photos of her set . . . multifloral central decal, accented with a burgandy stripe at the rim. Sets such as these are very rare! She also mentioned a set in red trimmed with gold and stamped 24 K Gold.

Bottom,

Left: This is the large footed salad bowl, decorated inside and out with lovely floral decals and piped in green . . . absolutely fantastic! (These decals and those on the dinnerware above are under-glazed, and were probably applied by the factory.)

Bottom,

Right: This 10" cake plate is completely flat and is very, very rare! It has been found in yellow, green and turquoise . . . perhaps we will find that it was made in the earlier six colors!

Top,

Left to Right: This creamer is 4″ high and was most probably experimental. The very unusual comport is only 10″ x 2½″ high. Next is the base section of the experimental individual tea pot we found in the morgue. We would have loved to show it with the lid, which is interchangeable with the A.D. pot, but this particular one was just enough "off-round" that our lid would not fit.

Bottom: These are unusual colors for the individual creamer and tray . . . both must be considered scarce, although not as extremely rare as we once thought. Only one sugar has been reported in any color other than the standard yellow; it is turquoise. Recently, a tray was reported in yellow.

The box containing a creamer features the Fiesta dancing girl. Advertising pieces such as this one are creating quite a stir!

The medium green small fruits are rare; the red relish section was designed so that four would fit a large oval tray — strictly experimental!

Upper
Left: This beautiful fruit comport with overall 22Kt gold decoration and multi floral decal was decorated by Royal China.

Center
Right: Gold rimmed and decorated with flowers, this relish is especially nice!

Center
Left: 8 pc. cake set, marked Georgian by Homer Laughlin. The Gold work was done by Royal China . . . the same decoration has been found on Fiesta chop plates and salad plates, also by Royal China.

Bottom
Right: George and Martha Washington grace this Bicentennial bowl and mug. The bowl is marked Rhythm, and on the reverse side of the mug: Washington Bicentennial (1732-1932).

Top: Bread box, garbage can

Bottom: Canister set, napkin holder

These tin items are decorated with Fiesta-like dinnerware of the type popular through the late 30's and into the 40's. The American Home, Oct. 1938, carried an article called "Pretty Up Your Kitchen" which featured not only Fiesta, but tinware by Owens-Illinois Can Co. decorated in "Roman stripes in red, blue, and green on yellow". The set consisted of canisters, tray, bread box, dust pan and garbage can, and it, too, was called "Fiesta". You may on occasion find tinware with the Mexicana decal!

"Fiesta" popcorn sets were marketed during the 1940's. They consisted of a large red round-bottomed bowl, and individual serving bowls in turquoise, green, yellow and navy enamel over tin. Fiesta-like rings were simulated in the metal near the rim of each piece.

Top: Paper items—especially advertising material—make interesting additions to our collections, and are really worthy investments! We wanted to show you the cover of this Saturday Evening Post, Oct. 10, '36, so that if the date escapes you, you will recognize this issue when you see it. Inside is a beautiful two-page Armstrong Floor covering ad with a vintage kitchen-dining room fairly blooming with Fiesta. (We would have photographed it for you, but a certain party, who shall remain name-less ruined her copy trying to decoupage it without first reading the instructions).

Another ad featuring Fiesta appeared in Better Homes and Gardens, Dec. 1936. The company's price lists not only contain much information, but are in themselves collectors items. The menu and the corn package are examples of the influence of HLC's lines in commercial work. The sheet of decals were produced in 1945 by a company called American Decalcomania of Chicago and New York, and sold for 29¢ per sheet of six designs. The glass decanter shown in two designs has been found, and is marked "Nolen Austin Co., Feb. 1942, Glasbake, Pat. U.S.A." You may find tiles in two sizes decorated with these decals.

Bottom: This full color display ad appeared in the Des Moines Register and Tribune on March 2, 1939. Only four basic colors were offered, so perhaps the set was keyed to the Mexican glassware tumblers . . . note the interesting blend of Fiesta and Riviera! These Fiesta Ensembles were assembled and shipped by Homer Laughlin. (See explanation, page 26.)

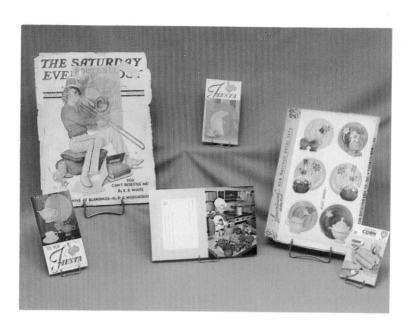

Top: Hankscraft Electric Egg Cooker. In the early 1940's the Hankscraft Company made and marketed their Electric Egg Cooker in service sets that included the cooker as shown here, "four vari-colored Fiesta egg cups, (red, yellow, blue and green), ivory (pottery) poaching dish, Fiesta salt and pepper shakers, and maple plywood tray". They called this set the "Fiesta Egg Service Set" and sold it for either $9.50 or $13.70 depending upon whose catalogue you happened to be using. (The lower price was from 1942, the higher from 1941, unlikely though that may seem in these days of 12% inflation!) The set shown at right has not been listed in any of these catalogues, but is the one more often found. Obviously, these are not Fiesta egg cups, but are made of the same material as the cooker itself, and are smaller than the Genuine Fiesta.

Bottom: HLC look-alikes! As we've tried to impress on new collectors, examine and study everything well before jumping to conclusions. We've included this photo to emphasize the point! On the right is a "Fiesta bud vase" that is not a Fiesta bud vase . . . but a copy of one. Aside from the obviously inferior glaze, the piece is just enough smaller to indicate that it has been made from a mold taken from an original. The disk pitcher is not!!! (and as Baretta would say, "dat's the name of dat tune"!) The cake plate, while very beautiful, is not Fiesta . . . the donkey may look like its Harlequin double, but sometimes pulls a cart marked "California"! A "dead ringer" without rings, the last pitcher looks very much like the Harlequin novelty creamer. Beware!

THE FIESTA CASUALS
GENUINE

H. L. Co. USA
CASUAL

There were two designs produced in the beautiful Fiesta Casuals; and although they are both relatively difficult to find, often, when they are available, the set may be complete, or nearly so.

They were first introduced in June, 1962; and, as sales were only moderately active, they were discontinued around 1968. The Plaid Stamp Company featured both of these designs in their illustrated catalogues during these years.

The Hawaiian 12-Point Daisy design, No. F-108, featured a ½″ turquoise band at the rim, and turquoise daisies with brown centers on a white background.

The other design was Yellow Carnation, No. F-107, which featured the yellow flowers with a touch of brown on the white background and with yellow piping at the rim. In both instances only the dinner plates, salad plates, saucers and oval platters were decorated; the cups, fruit dishes, nappies, and sugar and creamers were simply the matching Fiesta color.

Using a lead mask with the cut-out design, the decoration was hand-sprayed and overglazed. A complete service consisted of six place settings: dinner plate, salad plate, cup and saucer, and fruit (5½″). A platter, 8½″ nappy, and the sugar and creamer were also included.

AMBERSTONE

This "brown Fiesta" seems to have caused quite a stir among our collector friends; and it's easy to see why . . . especially when some of the hollowware pieces are found with the familiar Fiesta cast-indented trademark!

Amberstone was introduced in 1967, three years before the Fiesta line was restyled; yet the illustration on an old order blank shows that the sugar and creamer, cup, tea pot, soup/cereal, casserole, and coffee server were from the same molds that were later used for the Fiesta Ironstone. Only on the pieces that had relatively flat areas large enough to permit decoration do you find the black, machine-stamped underglazed pattern. The remainder were solid brown glazed.

Sold under the trade name of Genuine Sheffield dinnerware, it was produced by HLC exclusively for supermarket promotions, and several large grocery chains featured Amberstone as a premium. These items were offered, and for your information we have indicated those having the design with an asterisk:

Dinner Plate*
Dessert Dish
Bread & Butter*
Coffee Cup
Saucer*
Vegetable Bowl
Covered Sugar Bowl
Creamer
Oval Platter, 13"*
Large Soup Plate*
Ash Tray
Salt & Pepper Shakers
Salad Plate*

Soup/Cereal Bowl
Covered Casserole
Sauce Boat
Relish Tray*
Coffee Server
Tea Server
Covered Butter Dish, (stick)
Round Serving Platter*
Jumbo Salad Bowl
Covered Jam Jar
Serving Pitcher (disk)
Jumbo Mug
Pie Plate*

CASUALSTONE

In 1970, Homer Laughlin again produced a line of dinnerware to be sold exclusively as supermarket promotions. This dinnerware was called Casualstone, and was presented under the trade name "Coventry". The Antique Gold of the Fiesta Ironstone was decorated with an intricate gold machine stamped design and, as with Amberstone, it appeared on only the shallow items.

An old order blank shows that it was less expensive than the Amberstone of three years previous . . . and in these days of ever increasing inflation it was refreshing to notice this! But quite possibly this was due to the fact that a standard color was used. The following pieces were available; those with the design are indicated by an asterisk:

Dinner Plate*	Dessert Dish
Coffee Cup	Saucer*
Bread & Butter*	Round Vegetable Bowl
Covered Sugar Bowl	Creamer
13" Oval Platter*	Soup Plate*
Ash Trays	Salt and Pepper
Salad Plates*	Soup/Cereal Bowls
Covered Casserole	Sauce Boat
Relish Tray*	Coffee Server
Tea Server	Covered Butter Dish (stick)
Round Platter*	Jumbo Salad Bowl
Covered Jam Jar	Pitcher
Jumbo Mugs	Pie Plate*

FIESTA IRONSTONE

In 1969, Fiesta was restyled and the line that was offered in February 1970, was then called Fiesta Ironstone. There were many factors that, of necessity, brought this change about. Labor and production costs had risen sharply. Efforts to hold these costs down resulted in the use of two new colors which were, and still are, standard colors for several other lines of dinnerware produced at HLC, Antique Gold and Turf Green. This eliminated the need of a separate firing that had been necessary for the older Fiesta colors. It was pointed out to us as we toured the factory that since each color required different temperatures in the kiln, orders were running ahead of production on Fiesta as well as their other lines.

In order to cut labor costs, all markings were eliminated. (Only very occasionally will you find a marked item; this was never a practice and such pieces must be from the very early transition.)

The restyled pieces had a more contemporary feeling — bowls were flared; the applied handles were only partial rings. The covered casserole had molded, closed handles and the sugar bowl was without handles. The covered coffee server made a return appearance after an absence of several years.

Nineteen items were offered in three colors, Antique Gold, Turf Green, and the original red . . . now called Mango Red.

The oval platter was enlarged to 13"; two new items were offered, the sauceboat stand and a 10¼" salad bowl.

Finally in November, 1972, all production of Fiesta Red was discontinued because many of the original technicians who developed this color and maintained control over the complicated manufacturing and firing had retired and modern mass production methods were unsuited to the process.

Then at last, on January 1, 1973, the famous line of Fiesta Dinnerware was discontinued.

FIESTA KITCHEN KRAFT

Since the early 1930's the Homer Laughlin China Company had been well known as manufacturers of a wide variety of ceramic kitchen wares.

In 1939 they introduced a bake and serve line called Fiesta Kitchen Kraft, as an extension of their already popular genuine Fiesta ware. This they offered in the four original Fiesta colors — red, yellow, green and blue. The following pieces were available: (Compiled from April, 1941, price list)

> Covered Jars, small, medium and large
> Large covered Jug
> Mixing Bowls — 10", 8", and 6"
> Spoon, Fork and Cake Server
> Covered Casseroles, 8½", 7½", and individual
> 4 piece refrigerator set
> Pie plate, 10"
> Cake plate, 11"
> Large salt and pepper shakers
> Plates, 6" and 9"

These were chosen from the standard assortment of Kitchenware items which had been the basis of the many Kitchen Kraft and Oven Server decaled lines of years previous; none were created especially for Fiesta Kitchen Kraft.

This line was in production for a relatively short period, through the early '40's — perhaps being discontinued during the Second World War prior to 1945.

As collectors are becoming more aware of its identity, more of these Fiesta Kitchen Kraft items are becoming available. You undoubtedly know if you have collected it, it is by no means easily found, and prices are usually very high.

There were two standard marks used for this line — the cast indented mark and the paper label. Naturally, many of these paper labels were removed, and, as a result you will find many pieces are not marked. Occasionally you may find a third mark, simply Fiesta . . . hand stamped in gold ink.

In addition to the items listed previously, there are at least three more to add. These may have been offered in the original assortment and discontinued by the 1941 listing. The first of these to come to our attention was the oval platter. As with the casserole, it was supplied with a chrome holder, and shipped from the factory as a complete unit. There was also a chrome holder for the 10" pie plate. A second size pie plate measuring 9" has also been found. Although unmarked, it, too, is an easily recognizeable HLC mold, and is often found with decals in this size. As a good example of the durability of this kitchen ware, a good friend tells us of a relative who has used her pie plate once or twice a week for over thirty years, and it is still in very good condition!

The third new item is actually only a variation of one of those already listed, and has probably been the basis of more confusion and more questions than any other piece HLC ever made . . . and that is a second size Kitchen Kraft covered jug! The difference in size is so slight, even side by side it could go unnoticed — and to be honest, we don't know which size was the first, or which is the hardest to find. Collectors report as many of one size as the other. If you really want to label yours small or large, here are some measurements that will help you.

LARGE		SMALL
21½"	circumference	20"
5⅛"	base rim	4¾"
3¾"	rim inside lid	3⅜"
2⅜"	diameter of knob	2¼"

The 6″ and 9″ plates listed on the 1941 illustrated brochure were used as underplates for the hot casseroles. When we visited the morgue at HLC, we saw an example of these—they were of a thinner gauge and seemed to have been taken from one of their other lines, since the style was not typical . . . they were round and had a moderately wide, slightly flared rim. Although none have been reported in Fiesta KK colors, there is one shown with the Conchita KK in a later section.

If you have been interested at all in the decaled lines, you are probably familiar enough with the Kitchen Kraft molds, that you recognize them at first glimpse. Several collectors have mentioned finding the stack set, salt and peppers, mixing bowls and other items with an ivory glaze. As far as we can determine from any information available, ivory was never listed as a Fiesta KK color, so we assume the undecorated ivory ware was marketed under another line designation.

Bottom: Covered refrigerator jars. A unit consists of three stacking parts, with a flat lid . . . it's usually made up of all four Kitchen Kraft colors in the unit. This one is special!

Covered jugs! The smaller one stands 5⅞″ tall, the larger 6¼″. These are difficult to find in either size.

Trademarks:

Top: Casseroles, 8½″, 7½″, and individual. All sizes are very scarce; the small one is especially attractive to collectors, and they are usually priced quite high.

Middle: Covered jars; large, medium and small. Circumferences graduate from 27½″ to 22″, to 17¼″ on the small one. We now have three large jars — one blue, one red and one yellow — which we use as canisters . . . and lovely though they are, they just aren't very handy!

Bottom: These mixing bowls measure 10″, 8″, and 6″, and again have proven to be very difficult to find. Note the original sticker on the large one. They have been found in both Harlequin (lt. green, mauve blue and yellow) and Serenade colors (pink, blue/gray and gray). These sets have dry bases and are unsigned.

Although a Kitchen ware bowl seems an unlikely liquor decanter, the 6″ size has been reported with this message in gold underglaze lettering: "This whiskey is 4 years old, 90 proof Maryland straight rye whiskey, Wm. Jameson, Inc., N Y, SHOREWOOD, The finest name in rye".

Top: Cake plate. These may or may not be marked; the only decoration is the narrow band around the edge formed by one inverted ring.

Pie plates, 10″, 9″. The pie plates were produced without rings, either inside or outside, and are usually not marked. We have one with a gold ink stamp. The small size is very unusual to have been done in the Fiesta colors. This mold was more often decorated with decals.

Middle: On the left is the 10″ pie plate in the metal holder. The casserole in the center is the 8½″ and is shown in the metal holder, as shipped from HLC.

On the far right is the 13″ oval platter. These are extremely rare, and probably not marked. Of course, not all of these items were shipped with a metal holder.

Bottom: Spoon, fork and cake server. All are rated highly by collectors, and are not easily found. The handles are decorated with the same embossed flowers as one of the Oven Serve lines.

Salt and Peppers. Larger replicas of their original counterpart, although by no means as plentiful.

HARLEQUIN

Harlequin is a fascinating pattern, abundant with beautiful interesting pieces, as its many enthusiastic fans will be quick to tell you! Although it was first listed on company records in 1936, Harlequin was not introduced to the public until 1938. It was quite popular and sold very well into the late fifties when sales began to diminish. Records show that the final piece was actually manufactured in 1964.

Harlequin was produced by Homer Laughlin in their effort to serve all markets. It was a less expensive, thinner ware, and was sold without trademark exclusively by F. W. Woolworth Co. Stores.

The glaze was similar to Fiesta's, and all of Fiesta's lovely colors were used except ivory . . . but only a few rare pieces were made in dark blue. In addition, there was maroon, a mauve blue, and a "Blue Spruce" shade of green. Officially, the color we call "red" in Fiesta is "Tangerine" in the Harlequin line, and we learned from a retired employee that during some of the war years when uranium oxide was not available to make the standard red glaze, some Harlequin and Riviera was produced by means of a colored stain. The yellow is "Harlequin Yellow", according to the records, and the mauve simply blue. The "spruce" green color was called dark green, and was the original green, and they called the deep maroon shade "red"! If all this seems a bit confusing, may we suggest that to simplify matters (unless you are a purist, in which case "Good Luck"!) we collectors continue to call the Fiesta red shade "red", the spruce green shade "spruce green" rather than dark green since that name is commonly held to be interchangeable with Forest Green, the maroon color "maroon" rather than red which might just avoid an international incident if a Fiesta red fan were to get a maroon marmalade through a mail order instead of one in her beloved red! While your head is still spinning, may we add that although previously we felt that rose and salmon were one and the same, a recent conversation with an HLC spokesman revealed that there was once a shade called salmon — it was discontinued prior to the early 50's — and the rose color was a Harlequin 50's color, as it was in the

Fiesta line. Only rarely have we seen any Harlequin in a color that might qualify as salmon.

The following is an excerpt from one of the company's original illustrated brochures:

> "The new Harlequin Pottery offers a gift to table gaiety. It brings the magic of bright, exciting color to the table, dresses the festive board with pleasantness and personality, makes of every meal a cheerful and companionable occasion.
>
> The new ware comes in four lovely colors . . . Yellow, Green, Red, and Blue . . . and offers the hostess endless possibilities for creating interesting and appealing color effects on her table. All the colors are brilliant and eye-catching . . . designed to go together effectively in any combination the hostess may desire. To set a table with Harlequin is an adventure in decoration. Plates are of one color, cups of another, saucers and platters of another . . . you can give free range to your artistic instincts.
>
> And it is very easy to build up a comprehensive set of Harlequin in whatever items and colors you desire, because it may be bought by the piece at extremely reasonable prices.
>
> ### Sold Exclusively by
> ### F. W. WOOLWORTH CO. STORES"

The style of Harlequin is pure Art Deco. As with the Fiesta, the pattern consists of a band of concentric rings; however, on Harlequin these rings are spaced away from the rim by a plain margin, whereas with Fiesta the band is placed at the rim. Flat pieces are round and slightly concave, and there is no center motif. Many of the bowls are flared and complement the cone shape of the hollow-ware pieces. Handles are applied, slightly ornate at the base, and all are extremely angular with the exception of the service water jug and its twin in miniature, the novelty creamer.

The original line consisted of these items:

10″ plate
9″ plate
8″ soup plate
7″ plate
6″ plate
Salt and pepper shakers
Cream soup cup
9″ nappy
Sauceboat
Covered Casserole
A.D. (After Dinner) coffee cup and saucer
Novelty creamer
Tea cup and saucer
Creamer, regular
Sugar bowl
13″ platter
11″ platter
Tea pot
Service water jug
36's bowl
5½″ fruit
Ash tray
36's oatmeal
Double egg cup
Individual salad bowl
22 oz. jug
4½″ tumbler

The only written material the factory could provide, aside from the original brochure, is dated May 10, 1952. It lists both available and discontinued items, many of which were added to the original assortment over the intervening years.

Listed as discontinued:

Baker, 7″ (in the pottery trade, a baker is an oval vegetable)
Cov'd butter
Marmalade, cov'd
Individual nut bowl
Individual Creamer
Tankard
Relish Tray
Individual egg cup

In addition to those mentioned here, there are three more items that round out the list of unusual Harlequin pieces. The first is the ash tray saucer, the second a large cup...evidently the "tankard" on the discontinued list. It is styled with no rings and the sides are slightly curved rather than straight. It fits nicely into the ash tray saucer; in fact, a factory spokesman is sure they were intended to be used together. And the third, the individual creamer, 2¼″ tall...no rings—no angular lines—nothing to hint "Harlequin" except the colors! In a matching nut cup it looks like a tiny pitcher and bowl set, and a few dried star flowers and some status would make a dainty arrangement!

In 1939, the Hamilton Ross Co. offered a Harlequin look-alike which they called Sevilla. It came in assorted solid colors, eight in all, with the same angular handles, and similar style and decoration. The round platter was distinctive—it featured closed handles formed by the band of rings device which was allowed to sweep gradually outward to just past mid-point of the plate; no doubt you have seen an occasional piece.

In 1979, the Homer Laughlin Co. announced that they had been approached and would comply with a request from the F. W. Woolworth Company to reissue the Harlequin line, one of that company's all time best sellers, as a part of their one hundredth anniversary celebration. The Harlequin Ironstone dinnerware they produced was a very limited line and is easily recognized. It was made in three original colors—medium green, yellow, and turquoise and a new shade, coral. The sugar lid as well as the base was restyled with closed handles and a solid finial. A round platter, rather than the original oval, was included in the 45 pc. set, which was comprised of only plates, salad plates, cereal/soups, cups and saucers, sugar and creamer, and one vegetable bowl. The plates are backstamped Homer Laughlin (the old ones are not) and even the pieces made with authentic molds are easy to distinguish from old Harlequin. Considering the many lovely colors of the original line and that virtually none of its unique accessory pieces were reproduced, this late line should cause little if any concern to the many collectors who love Harlequin dinnerware.

Top: 10″ plate in spruce, 9″ in rose, 7″ in mauve, and 6″ in turquoise. The larger plate is becoming very hard to find, and the 9″ is by no means plentiful!

Center: Platters, 13″ and 11″.

Bottom: 8″ soup plate, 36's oatmeal shown in med. green, 6½″, 5½″ fruit, and cream soup.

The 36's oatmeal may be a little hard to find, and although the cream soups are around, they seem to be scarce in dark green, grey, rose and chartreuse. The trend toward medium green is as evident in Harlequin as it is in Fiesta.

Note: The small incised letters and/or numbers sometimes found on the bottom of hollowware pieces were used to identify a pieceworker . . . perhaps a molder or a trimmer . . . and were used for quality control purposes. More likely to appear on Harlequin, nevertheless these are sometimes seen on Fiesta as well.

Opposite: 9″ nappy in red, 36's bowl in yellow, 9″ oval baker in mauve blue, 7″ individual salad bowl, here shown in grey.

The casserole is a beautiful example of the styling in the Harlequin line; and, although you might have to search for awhile for one, they are to be found.

As a general rule, you will find less med. green, chartreuse, grey, and dark green in the Harlequin line . . . and the casserole is no exception — it's scarce in these colors, too. Rose and red Harlequin seem to be in ample supply. The 36's bowl is very hard to find in rose, grey, chartreuse, med. green and dark green; and the individual salad bowls are scarce in dark green, rose and red.

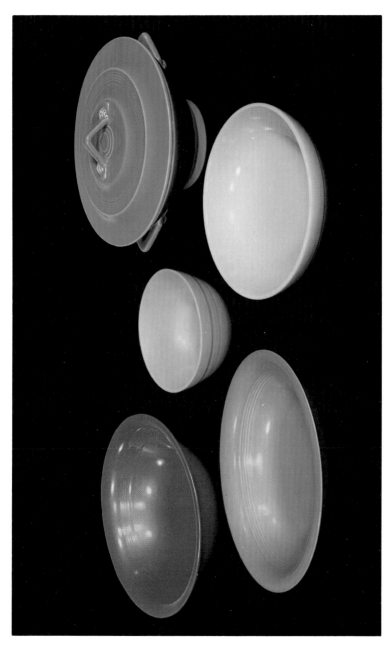

Top: Notice the band of rings near the bottom on the water jug. This will help you identify this jug as Harlequin. Shown with the water tumblers . . . doesn't it make a beautiful set? As you can plainly see . . . the band of rings are spaced away from the rim by a plain margin, whereas, on the Fiesta tumblers, the rings are at the rim. This has caused some confusion, and often collectors of one pattern have been disappointed with mail orders, when tumblers of the other pattern have been mistakenly represented. Harlequin tumblers are harder to find than Fiesta tumblers. To our knowledge, neither pitcher or tumblers have been found in grey, chartreuse or med. green, and they're quite scarce in light green, rose and maroon.

Bottom: Tea pot, tea cups and saucers. Aren't the cups elegant! There's just no way to hold that dainty handle, without having your "pinkie" automatically extend just a little!

Top: Sugar with cover, and regular creamer, salt and pepper. To the left are two unusual creamers, 3" high . . . notice the difference in the length of the lips on the two shown. This is due to the fact that it was trimmed by hand. These are very hard to find! The novelty creamer is shown in red, you'll rarely find it in med. green, chartreuse, dark green or grey. The maroon piece is the marmalade; yellow and turquoise are common; spruce, red, rose, and mauve are harder to come by.

Bottom: Sauceboat; tumbler with decal of antique car is one of a set of 6, decorated by Pearl China. The 22 oz. jug on the left is especially hard to find in dark green, medium green, grey and chartreuse.

Top: The maroon ash tray-saucer combination is shown on the far left. These are very hard to find. Above, in turquoise, is the little basketweave nut dish. At the top of the photo is the rare Harlequin syrup . . . only a few are known to exist. Below it is the ash tray. Note that the rings on this pattern are inside the bowl, rather than on the top rim as Fiesta's are. The large cup, or tankard, is shown to the right of the ash tray. These are very rare. Although we once thought the basketweave ash tray was only an experimental item, too many have been found to support this idea. Chartreuse and dark green are scarce colors, but "status" red tops the price scale.

The little perfume bottle was a specially-made item for a cosmetic company. The butter dish, shown in spruce, originally was part of the Century line, and was dipped in Harlequin colors to be sold with this line and Riviera. These colors are available: cobalt blue, rose, mauve, spruce, light green, maroon, turquoise, "Tangerine" red, yellow and ivory.

Bottom: 5 part relish tray. The base is identical to the Fiesta relish tray, only the rings are slightly altered. It is really a beautiful piece!

Strangely enough, the only true Harlequin bases have been turquoise! When another color is used, they have been done on Fiesta bases!

To the right is an example of a common practice . . . some enterprising company turned a 36's bowl into a nut dish, with the addition of a little chrome and a glass knob!

Recently, a collector sent us a photo of the first Harlequin tiered tid-bit we've heard of . . . very nice!

Top: Double egg cups, here shown in chartreuse, are not hard to find, except in the rare colors, but red ones are becoming scarce. The individual egg cup, shown in spruce, was in production only a short time . . . probably because the stems were hand turned and trimmed . . . and are quite rare. The Harlequin candleholders, too, are rare. The A.D. (after dinner) cups and saucers are styled exactly like the tea cups, and are becoming hard to find—especially in dark green, grey and chartreuse, but most difficult in medium green, which is considered by many as the "prime" color in Harlequin.

Bottom: Spoon rests have always created quite a stir (absolutely no pun intended). We thought at first they belonged to the Fiesta family, but later we learned that they were Harlequin. Then, if there was any remaining doubt about it, this beautiful turquoise example was found with its "Harlequin" label intact! The second one is an advertising item. These are often found in white with various colorful decals. Their measurements are 8¼" × 6¼".

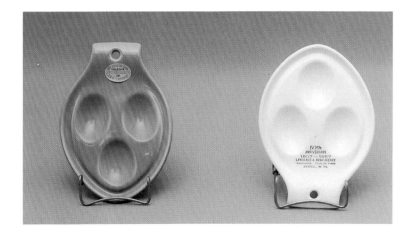

Top: This wire frame donkey carries Harlequin salt and peppers in his saddlebags — not a HLC product, but cute! In the center is the petite newcomer to the line, the individual creamer. It's 2¼" high and you'll find them in turquoise, mauve blue, spruce green, maroon, yellow, light green, red, and rose. The metal holder turns the tumbler into a tall mug.

Bottom: The cup is the rare tankard, and although the saucer is much larger than the standard Rhythm saucer (this one is 6⅞") the styling is identical. Probably one of a kind, the lamp in the center has a base from a large Fiesta comport, a body of two Harlequin casseroles, and the neck is a small Fiesta comport stem. The Harlequin pamphlet introduces the new line, but lists no prices or assortment. It does name the original colors, yellow, green (spruce), red (maroon) and blue (mauve). Although today we all seem to prefer matching cups and saucers, the pamphlet suggests the buyers be more adventurous . . . it recommends "cups of one color, saucers of another."

HARLEQUIN ANIMALS

This menagerie of darling animals is part of the Harlequin line. They were sold through F. W. Woolworth Co. Stores during the late 30's, perhaps very early in the 40's, when miniatures such as these were enjoying a hey-day. They are quite rare! For our photography session, a whole herd of the animals arrived — each of the six represented in all four colors . . . maroon, spruce, mauve and yellow . . . plus gold, and white with gold trim!

In the top photo are the original HLC Harlequin animals in authentic glazes. There are no others, although this wee clique has been besieged by hordes of little deer, elephants, other ducks — even a cart — trying to squirm into line. True, the little duck has a double — a perpetually hungry little gander, his head bent into a permanent feeding position — but he was made by the Brush Pottery Company! And although several collectors were almost sure their 2½″ elephant was a "charter member", HLC disowned him! The cart we mentioned is pulled by a donkey "look-alike" (but a second look shows an uncharacteristic lack of sharp detail) and has been found to occasionally bear a "California" mark!

The bottom photo displays the "Maverick" animals . . . a most appropriate term adopted by collectors to indicate animals that have been altered by someone outside the Homer Laughlin China Company. Those in the double row at the bottom are of the same size as the original animals. In some cases, the gold finish or the gold and white finish has been applied over a Harlequin colored glaze. One company involved in decorating the animals was Kaulware, of Chicago, who utilized an iridescent glaze and gold hand painted trim. On the top row of the bottom photo are examples of salt and pepper shakers of a slightly smaller size, which indicates they have been made from molds made from the original animals . . . in fact one of the penguins is a bit smaller than the other.

Only lately, two red cats have been reported . . . no doubt resulting from the whim of an employee!

RIVIERA

Riviera was introduced by HLC in 1938 and was sold exclusively by the Murphy Co. In contrast to Fiesta and Harlequin, the line was quite limited. It was unmarked, lighter weight, and therefore less expensive. Very rarely, a piece may be found with the Homer Laughlin gold ink stamp.

Of the three colored dinnerware lines, Riviera has the rather shaky distinction of being the only one which was not originally created as such. Its forerunner was a line called Century — an ivory line with a vellum glaze. Century shapes were also decorated with a wide variety of decals and were the basis of many lines, such as Mexicana and Hacienda. The butter dish was used in the Virginia Rose pattern. An enterprising designer applied the popular colored glazes to these same shapes, and Riviera was born! Even the shakers were taken from another line. They were originally designed as Tango — which accounts for the six section design in contrast to the square Riviera shape.

Riviera is in very short supply, and much to the chagrin of Riviera collectors everywhere, mint condition pieces are very few indeed. Especially bad to chip, were the flat pieces . . . plates, platters, saucers, and undersides of lids. Still, when it is found with no chips, the glaze is nearly always in beautiful condition.

The style is very functional . . . the cups especially so. It is square and somewhat squatty, yet it has so much quaint charm. Certainly Riviera will endear itself to many!

Colors are mauve blue, red, yellow, light green and ivory. On rare occasions dark blue pieces are found . . . but this was never listed as a standard Riviera color. However, there is one thing we have learned — anything is apt to turn up, color-wise! Vats containing upwards of fourteen different colors were all around. Human error and innovation resulted in many unusual things!

Records for this line are especially scanty; but, as accurately and completely as possible, here is a listing of the items in the line as it was first introduced:

8″ dish (platter)
10″ dish (platter)
8″ plate
7″ plate
5″ plate
Tea cups and saucers
Fruit
7″ baker (oval vegetable bowl)
Salt and pepper shakers
Covered casserole
Deep plate
7″ nappy
6″ Oatmeal
Tumblers (with handle)
Open Jug (also found with lid)
Tea Pot
Sauceboat
Creamer
Covered sugar

We have also found a 10″ dinner plate, 15″ platters, a covered syrup pitcher and two sizes of butter dishes . . . a half lb., and a quarter lb. There is also a juice set, (jug and tumblers), and recently a demmitasse cup and saucer has been discovered. These are all extremely hard to find.

Although it is uncertain just when Riviera was discontinued, it was sometime prior to 1950. Riviera is a challenge to collect; but you can be sure the effort will be worthwhile!

Top: 10″ dinner plates are very hard to come by! 9″ luncheon, 7″ bread and butter, shown in dark blue which is very unusual in this line (we have seen one other piece) and 6″ dessert bowl. *Tole Painters:* All sizes make lovely·wall decorations!

Center: Two styles of platters, one with no handles, and one with closed handles. The light green one measures 11½″, the mauve blue one, 11¼″.

Bottom: Two more platters, 13¼″ and 12″. This is the other piece of cobalt blue that we know of. Notice that the wells in these two platters are square, and in the two above, the wells are oval.

The 13¼″ platter has also been found with an oval well, also a 15½″ one with an oval well.

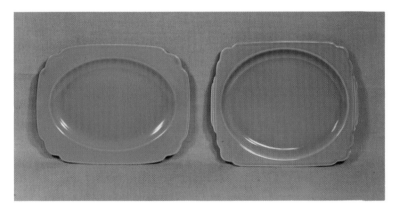

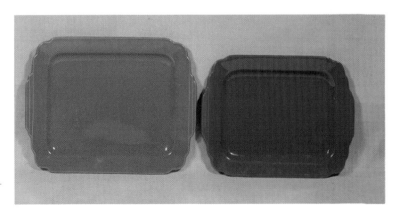

Top: Tea pot, tea cups and saucers. We had a red cup that would have added a beautiful accent to the photo, but, alas, no saucer! Since then, we have received one as a gift from a thoughtful friend!

Bottom: In the top row, from left to right, you see a blue 5½″ fruit; a 9¼″ yellow baker with curving sides, and a soup plate, 8″.

In the lower left corner of the photo, there is a 9″ baker, with straight sides. The red nappy in the right corner measures 8¼″.

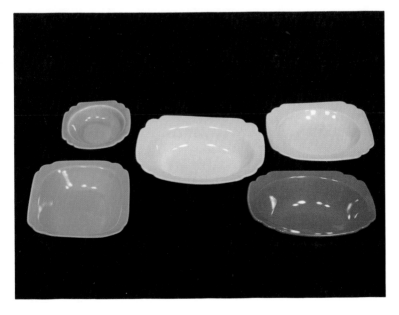

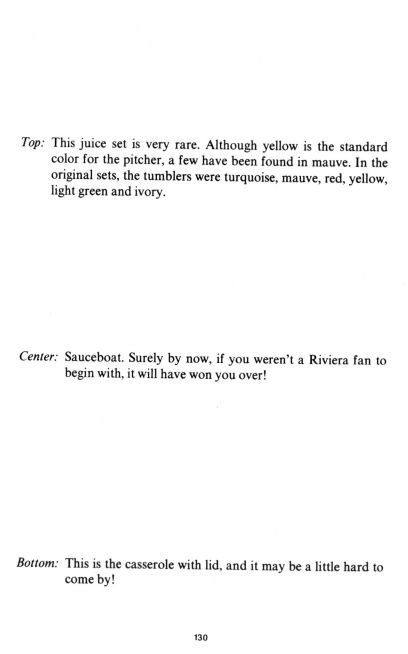

Top: This juice set is very rare. Although yellow is the standard color for the pitcher, a few have been found in mauve. In the original sets, the tumblers were turquoise, mauve, red, yellow, light green and ivory.

Center: Sauceboat. Surely by now, if you weren't a Riviera fan to begin with, it will have won you over!

Bottom: This is the casserole with lid, and it may be a little hard to come by!

Shown here is the covered jug, surrounded by four colors of the handled tumblers. The jugs are really quite hard to find, and have been found with cover in only light green and ivory. Below are the salt and pepper shakers. As you can see, there are six orange-like segments that make up the design . . . these were borrowed from the Tango line . . . yet they are compatible with the other Riviera pieces. Two pair have been found in a true red glaze . . . origin unconfirmed.

In the center of the picture are the two sizes of butter dishes. The large one holds a half lb., and they are much easier to find than the smaller quarter lb. size. The larger one is available in mauve, rose, yellow, spruce, light green, turquoise, maroon, dark blue, and red.

To the right are the regular creamer and sugar; above is the little covered syrup pitcher . . . a darling piece and rather rare.

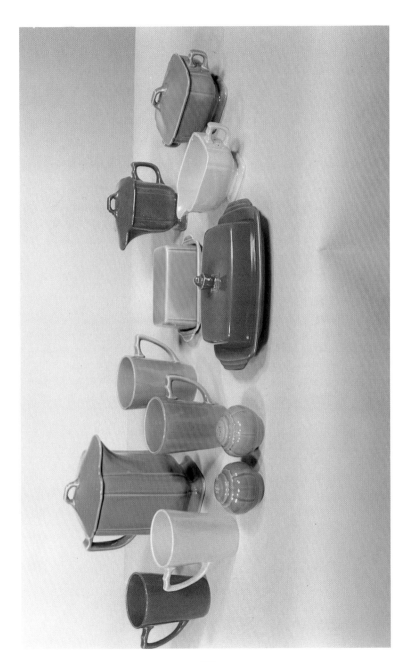

Top: The batter set, complete with tray in cobalt, covered syrup pitcher and the tall covered jug — used for mixing, storing and pouring the batter for pancakes. These complete sets are quite unique, since they utilize one of the very rare cobalt blue pieces found in Riviera, and the cover for the tall jug — another hard to find item. In fact, the little covered syrup pitcher is also scarce.

Bottom: These tumblers are 4″ and 5¼″ tall and feature a band of Riviera Mauve. A collector has reported similar glassware styled with vertically paneled sides trimmed with one band of color — light green, mauve, yellow or red — at the rim. Bought at auction with a set of Riviera, the glassware was still in the original box marked "Juanita Beverage Set", Rosenthal and Ruben, Inc., Binghampton, N.Y., 1938. There are two each of the four colors in four different sizes of tumblers: 3″, 3½″, 4″ and 5¼″. Matching swizzle sticks complete the 48 piece set.

The demitasse cup and saucer is from the Century line, the forerunner of Riviera. Although only ivory has been reported, HLC indicates that they were produced in solid colors and sold with Riviera. One lucky collector has a set with the Mexicana decals.

135

Top: Borrowing a Century plate, this Dick Tracy child's set is rare and very collectable! One such set has been found still packed in its original carton! According to the backstamp, it was made in 1950.

Bottom: Sure to become a "must" on everyone's "want list", this HLC child's set is beautifully done in colorful detailed decals on ivory. This set and many other items often carry an ink stamped series of letters and numbers; the Company has provided this information that should be of help to you in deciphering these codes:

"In 1900 the trademark featured a single numeral identifying the month, a second single numeral identifying the year and a numeral 1, 2, or 3 designating the point of manufacture as East Liverpool, Ohio.

In the period 1910-20, the first figure indicated the month of the year, the next two numbers indicated the year, and the third figure designated the plant. Number 4 was "N", Number 5 was "N5", and the East End plant was "L".

A change was made for the period of 1921-1930. The first letter was used to indicate the month of the year such as "A" for January, "B" for February, "C" for March. The next single digit number was used to indicate the year and the last figure for the plant.

For the period 1931-40 the month was expressed as a letter, but the year was indicated with two digits. Plant No. 4 was "N", No. 5 was "R", No. 6 and 7 were "C", and No. 8 was listed as "P". During the period, E-44R5 would indicate May of 1944 and manufactured by Plant No. 5. The current trademark has been in use for approximately 70 years, and the numbers are the only indication of the year that items were produced."

Top: "Tom Thumb and the Butterfly". A darling HLC child's set! On the front of the cereal bowl, Tom is chased by a Dragon fly, on the back, Tom is talking with a turtle. What a shame these are so rare—every collector should have a set!

Bottom: Shown is only one place setting from a service for four— a gift to us from collector friends here in our "Hoosier" State. The shapes are "Rhythm by Homer Laughlin" and each piece is so marked, except for the cups. According to the dating code, they were made in 1954 . . .we have never seen another piece!

139

DECALED CENTURY

These are only a few examples of the many different decal decorations applied to Century shapes by Homer Laughlin. Many carry the particular name of the line on the back, and the year of manufacture is often represented by a dating code. Many collectors are fascinated by these decaled lines and have reassembled their favorite patterns into lovely, entire sets.

9″ plates, Old English Scene, Columbine and Briar Rose. The last two patterns in particular have become quite popular.

13″ platter with gold decoration; 11″ platter in the Petipoint pattern.

This 12″ advertising platter with beautiful rose decal is stamped "L. Linsenberg, Meats, Groceries, Bakers, 217 E. Main St., Morristown, Pa." In the center, a scarce 15½″ platter with a square well; its backstamp indicates a 1933 manufacture. The 10½″ platter with oval well is very rare.

141

VIRGINIA ROSE

"Virginia Rose" was the name given a standard HLC shape, and it was used from 1929 into the 70's as a basis for more than a dozen lines of patterned dinnerware. To help us better understand this varied line, here is HLC's statement:

> Virginia Rose is a shape name that incidentally was named for the daughter of our top management official at that time. This possibly has been our most popular line ever produced and was responsible for the construction of our plant #8, the world's largest single pottery at that time, basically to produce the Virginia Rose line. This plant began operations in 1929 and the shape was finally discontinued in the early 70's. Even now the same shape has been adopted by our hotel division and currently is one of the best selling shapes in the hotel and institutional field. There were many many decorations including decal with or without lines as well as patterns applied with air brushes through lead masks on the Virginia Rose shape. At that time all patterns were merely identified by number each preceded by the capital VR and a series of three numerals as the idea of applying a name to dinnerware decoration by manufacturers has merely been developed in recent years.

Shown here is one of the more collectable lines:

Top, row 1: 11½" platter, 10½" dinner plate, 10½" platter,
    Row 2: 8½" vegetable bowl, 9" plate, 10½" covered casserole
    Row 3: 7½" vegetable bowl, 9½" platter, 8" plate 8" deep plate

Bottom, row 1: 7" plate, 5" milk pitcher, double egg cup, 6" plate
    Row 2: Sauce boat, ½ lb. butters with variations in decal, covered sugar
    Row 3: Creamer, mug, deep bowl

143

Top, row 1: 11½" platter, 15½" platter, 3 nested mixing bowls

Row 2: 8" Kitchen Kraft casserole, 9½" pie plate, 8" oval vegetable

Row 3: 5" fruit, 9" vegetable, salt and pepper, cup and saucer, 6" oatmeal

Bottom: We thought these nested mixing bowls were especially nice. The orange tree pattern is very similar to the one used by Fenton! They're marked with the HLCo mark, and have also been found in yellow.

RHYTHM ROSE

Rhythm Rose—beautiful rose decoration often on standard Rhythm shapes, although some items are "borrowed" from other HLC lines. It was produced from the mid-forties through the mid-fifties, and is marked with the gold stamp: Household Institute, Rhythm Rose.

Top, row 1: 9″ dinner plate, 10½″ cake plate, 9″ KK underplate

Row 2: Open KK jug pitcher, 8″ deep plate, 8½″ KK casserole

Row 3: A. D. cup and saucer marked Egg shell (a 25% lighter, 25% stronger body), decorated with gold at rim by "Eastern China, NY, U.S.A., 22K Gold", (stamped in gold on saucer); 9½″ KK pie plate; sauceboat

Front: The cake server is also decorated in 22K gold by "Kings Quality Fine Dinnerware"

Bottom, row 1: 6″ plate, KK coffee pot, set of 3 KK nested mixing bowls, KK coffee pot (note decal), 6″

Row 2: KK underplate
Tea pot, 13″ platter, sugar and creamer

Not shown are cups and saucers, fruits, oatmeals, vegetable bowls. No doubt you will find other items. Considered a "real prize" (and understandably so) by its owners—a "Harlequin" spoon rest in Rhythm Rose!

PRISCILLA PATTERN DINNERWARE

Only one of the many beautiful patterns of dinnerware fast becoming very collectable. As the photo indicates, this lovely line was offered with a wide assortment of serving pieces.

DOGWOOD

This lovely line of HLC dinnerware was produced in the early 1960's and is decorated with delicate sprigs of flowering dogwood.

149

SERENADE

Serenade was a pastel dinnerware line that was produced for only about three years in the early 40's. It was offered in four lovely pastel shades — yellow, green, pink and blue. Although not well accepted by the public when it was introduced, today's collectors find its soft delicate hues and dainty contours appealing. The pink bowl is a Kitchen Kraft casserole bottom, and is marked in the mold "Serenade". In addition to the pieces shown in the photo, these items were offered: deep plates, lug soups, pickles, platters, sauceboats and teapots.

JUBILEE

Jubilee was presented in 1948 by The Homer Laughlin China Company to celebrate their 75th year of ceramic leadership. The shape was simple, yet sophisticated, and the colors were Celedon Green, Shell Pink, Mist Grey and Cream Beige. The Jubilee calendar plate is dated 1953. The reverse side of the price list is reproduced below.

150

TANGO

Tango was a line introduced in the late 1930's . . . it was offered in blue, green, yellow and red. A price list dated 1937 indicates that it was sold through McLellan Stores Company, in New York City. In addition to the pieces shown in the photo, these were also listed: bakers, covered casseroles, creamers, covered sugars, dishes, fruits, nappies, and plates, 8" and 7".

RHYTHM

Rhythm was introduced at approximately the same time as the Harlequin line, and continued in production at least through the early 50's, perhaps even beyond. The color assortment listed on a 1952 price list reads: Harlequin yellow, chartreuse, grey, green, and burgandy . . . you may find others. In addition to those in the photo, stock items included nappies, 7"; fruits, 4"; plates, 4" and 7"; pickle dish; 8" dish; cream and covered sugar; sauceboat; teapot; casserole and cover (or nappy cover); and salt and pepper.

Competition was fierce among the large rival dinnerware companies. No sooner had a new idea been introduced to the public by one, than another company offered a similar product. Serenade and Jubilee were less than successful attempts to edge out T S & T's very popular Lu Ray Pastels . . . Ballerina, by Universal Potteries, Cambridge, O, was very much like Rhythm in color and styling; and their pastel line was "Laurella". Mt. Clemens Pottery sold a solid color dinnerware whose classic colonial style is very much like Tango's.

153

HOMER LAUGHLIN MEXICANA
. . . the Pattern that Started A Vogue

. . . so reads a trade paper from May, 1938 . . .

"When this Homer Laughlin pattern was first exhibited last July at the House Furnishing Show, it was an immediate smash hit. Its popularity has grown steadily ever since . . . and retailers have found it a constant and dependable source of profit. It started the vogue for the Mexican motif in crockery decoration which has since swept the country.

"And small wonder! For this Mexicana pattern is smart, colorful and attractive. It embodies the old-world atmosphere of Mexico with the modern verve and personality which is so appealing to American housewives. Applied to the pleasing, beautifully designed Homer Laughlin shapes, it presents a best seller of the first order."

Top: You will often find this line marked ''Mexicana'' with a gold backstamp. Although occasionally found with yellow, green and blue bands, red is by far the most plentiful. The Mexican motif tumblers are as compatible with these lines as they are with Fiesta, Harlequin or Riviera.

Bottom: 10" plate, 13" platter, 9" plate
Sauceboat, 9" oval vegetable, cup and saucer
Sauce boat liner, covered sugar and creamer

154

155

Nor was HLC the only company to 'jump on the band-wagon'—Paden City, Vernon Kiln, Crown, Stetson and many others produced similarly decorated lines with a decided Mexican flavor. Homer Laughlin themselves offered several. Besides Mexicana, Hacienda and Conchita (all decaled Century lines and perhaps their best known), they also made Arizona, decorated with a large green cactus, adobe house, yucca plant and pottery jug on an ivory glaze . . . and an unidentified ware (shown on right) that utilized the company's Yellowstone shape and featured pottery jugs and jars, cacti and a siesta-taking Mexican snoozing under his sombrero. This line has been dubbed Max-i-cana by collectors, and is by no means easy to come by!

Top, row 1: Mexicana. 8″ deep plate, 11″ platter, 7″ plate
Row 2: 6″ oatmeal, 8″ vegetable bowl, 6″ plate
Row 3: 5″ nappy, 4¾″ lug soup

Bottom, row 1: Max-i-cana. 11½″ platter, 13½″ platter, 10″ platter
Row 2: Creamer; egg cup (Torpeda shape); sugar; egg cup (top and bottom slightly rolled, shape name unknown); 8½″ casserole with lid; tripod candleholders marked Fiesta*
Front: 8½″ sauce boat liner

*Matching fruit comport, footed salad bowl, and bulb candleholders have also been found . . . watch for other Fiesta with these red stripes!

This type of dinnerware became popular during the late 30's; but from the dating codes found on these items, we can conclude that production lasted until near the end of the next decade— quite a long run for so bold a theme!

"Max-i-cana", Yellowstone mold

> *Top, row 1:* 6″ plate, 7″ plate, sauceboat
> *Row 2:* 4½″ lug soup, 8½″ vegetable bowl, cup and saucer

> *Bottom, row 1:* 9″ plate, 9½″ plate, 6″ plate
> *Row 2:* 9½″ vegetable bowl, 8″ deep plate
> *Row 3:* 6″ oatmeal, ½ lb. butter/cover, 5″ fruit

Hacienda! The tea pot is very rare, and a butter dish has been reported.

Top, row 1: 9" plate, 11" platter with square well, 6" plate
Row 2: Creamer, covered sugar, tea pot with lid, sauceboat
Row 3: Cup and saucer, 5" fruit

Bottom, row 1: 11½" platter with oval well, 13½" platter with oval well, 8" deep plate
Row 2: 8" vegetable bowl, 10" dinner plate, 9" vegetable bowl
Row 3: 8" casserole in Natulis shape, white glaze (a covered sugar has been reported in this shape and color, you may find other items); 6" oatmeal

Top: The tablecloth and napkins are of the same vintage . . . the multicolored tumblers show both sides of one decorated with Spanish dancers; and the one in the center shows the Genuine Fiesta dancing girl! On the right is the popular Mexicana pattern on a shape called Swing—by far the hardest of the Mexican lines to find!

Center: Conchita dinnerware (marked occasionally with line name in gold)

> 11½" platter, 13½" platter, 8" deep plate
> 5" dessert, 9" plate, 8" vegetable bowl
> Covered sugar, creamer, cup and saucer

KITCHEN KRAFT AND OVEN SERVE

From the very early 1930's Homer Laughlin China was the leading manufacturer of a very successful type of oven-to-table kitchen wares. These lines were called Oven-Serve and Kitchen Kraft. The variety of items offered and the many patterns and decaled lines that were made allow for an endless field of interest for collectors today.

Bottom: Conchita Kitchen Kraft. Although quite rare, you will probably find other examples of this line.

> *Row 1:* Large covered jar, large mixing bowl, medium covered jar
> *Row 2:* Covered jug, 10½" cake plate, 8" casserole, 9" underplate

Kitchen Kraft Mexicana . . . a line very popular with collectors! You may also find, in addition to the examples shown here, the small and medium jars, small and medium mixing bowls, and the individual casserole.*

Top, row 1: 10″ pie plate, 10″ mixing bowl
    Row 2: Spoon, pie server, fork; 8½″ casserole; salt and peppers

Bottom, row 1: Large covered jar, 10½″ cake plate, covered jug
    Row 2: Salt and pepper shakers, two units of the stack refrigerator jars with lid

*No Kitchen Kraft Hacienda has ever been reported.

Top: Aren't these ivory Kitchen Kraft items lovely decorated with delicate floral decals! The jug is rarely found with a cover in these decaled lines.

Row 1: Medium and small covered jars
Row 2: Large covered jar, stack refrigerator jars with lid, covered jug
Row 3: Individual casserole with lid, refrigerator jar with lid

Bottom: Kitchen Kraft with Tulips, marked KK Oven Serve
Row 1: Large covered jar; 10½″ cake plate; small, medium and large nested bowls
Row 2: Medium jar, 14½″ fruit bowl (extremely rare), 8½″ casserole with lid in metal holder
Row 3: Small covered jar, cake server, 9½″ pie plate, salt and pepper

Top: These matching pieces must have been a housewife's delight. Here are the 10″ mixing bowl, 10″ pie plate and server . . .they're all marked Kitchen Kraft, Oven Serve.

Bottom: Embossed line, Oven Serve. This is the line that carries the embossed floral pattern that decorates the handles of the Fiesta Kitchen Kraft spoon, fork and server. Shown on the top row, left to right: 7″ round bowl, 8½″ casserole, 6″ mixing bowl with floral decal. Bottom Row: 8″ oval baker, 9″ plate with multicolor design underglaze, custard cup, and 5¾″ turquoise fruit. You will occasionally find other colored glazes and various decal treatments on these shapes. This was quite an extensive line, and many unique pieces were produced. Watch for an almost identical line by T.S.&T.

Guaranteed
To Withstand Changes of
Oven-Dinner Ware
"THE OVEN WARE FOR TABLE SERVICE"
The Homer Laughlin China Co.
Newell, W. Va.

This label was found on a spoon and fork in a tan-gold glaze.

Top: We personally love the decaled pie plates. These are 10″ plates, in perfect condition and really quite beautiful!

Middle: This pattern is called Kitchen Bouquet . . . wouldn't it add a cheerful note to the kitchen! Shown are the 10″ pie plate, and the 13″ oval Kitchen Kraft platter. You may find these in the metal holders, too.

Bottom: Matching cake plate, 11″ deep dish pie plate, and server. Absolutely beautiful! These type pieces are not too easily found, rarely at a bargain.

171

THE AMERICAN POTTER

As a tribute to the American Potter, six pottery companies united their efforts and jointly built and operated an actual working kiln at the 1939-40 World's Fair in New York. A variety of plates, vases, figural items and bowls in a myriad of colors were produced — these were marked with an ink stamp "The American Potter, 1939 (or 40), World's Fair Exhibit, Joint Exhibit of Capitol and Labor."

The Homer Laughlin China Company entry—proudly designed by Rhead—is shown in the top photo. In the center of each plate, you can see the Trylon and the Parisphere, adopted symbols of the Fair. One of these has been found with this commemorative message stamped in gold on the back:

"Decorated by Charles Murphy, 150th Anniversary Inauguration of George Washington as First President of the United States, 1789-1939.

In the bottom photo are the entries from the other five companies. The cake set is from The Cronin China Co., Minerva O, National Brotherhood of Operative Potters. The 10" bowl in the center is marked Paden City Pottery, Made In USA, and the 10¾" plate on the right is marked Knowles, Joint Exhibit of Capitol and Labor. The smaller piece is actually the bottom half of a marmalade, and is embossed with the Trylon and Parisphere and the words "New York World's Fair". It's 3" tall and is marked "Edwin M. Knowles, China Co., Semi Vitreous".

Although not mentioned on the original pamphlet with the other companies and their entries, the pitcher is a World's Fair souvenir marked Porcelier Trade Mark, Vitreous Hand Decorated China, Made in U.S.A.

Top: The Potters' Plates are possibly the easiest of the World's Fair items to find. There were two — on the left. The Potter at His Wheel; and the companion plate on the right — The Artist Decorating the Vase. Turquoise and Light Green have also been found. Of course, to find one in the original box would be most unusual. Also shown is a cup and saucer embossed with signs of the Zodiac . . . another rarity!

Bottom: This is a beautiful display of hand turned vases — especially the small ones are becoming very popular. They are from 1½" to 2¾" high and all are marked with the ink stamp. The larger vases are from 5" to 7" tall; the cobalt blue piece on the far right is a candleholder. Note the red individual creamer from the Harlequin line, "World's Fair" etched on the side.

175

Top: Experimental ware from the family of Lloyd Dittmer, Ceramic Engineer at HLC during the years of Fiesta's development. The red and cobalt blue Potters plates were never mass produced.

Bottom: These plates and ashtray are souvenirs of the Golden Gate International Exposition of 1939 & 1940. They are marked Golden Gate Intern. Expo., Copyrighted License 63C, Homer Laughlin (Souvenir)

Top: Two figural pitchers, each 5″ tall. Martha Washington is marked The American Potter, New York World's Fair, with the year 1940 on a raised disk superimposed over a Trylon. George Washington is marked First Edition For Collectors, Limited to 100 Pieces, The American Potter, New York's World Fair, 1939. It is numbered 37. The tall vase measures 7″ and is marked with the ink stamp.

On the second row, the Martha and George Washington pitchers are each 2″ tall and are marked. These are sometimes found in bisque, and one pair in mauve blue has been reported.

The toothpick holder in the center is 2″ high; the salt and pepper shakers are 2½″ . . . neither are marked.

Bottom: The four season plates are 4¼″ across:
Spring shows a man fishing for trout;
Summer depicts a family picnicking;
Autumn shows a man hunting with his dog;
and Winter, a couple skating.

179

In the early 1900's, evidently attempting to enter the art pottery field, the Homer Laughlin China Company produced a unique line of art china. It was marked in gold with the eagle and the line name, Laughlin Art China. Examples of this ware are very rare. They are characteristically very colorful and are usually gold trimmed.

And so there seems to be no end to this area of collecting fun! At first we were strictly "Fiesta collectors", who soon discovered Harlequin . . . and Riviera . . . Amberstone . . . World's Fair . . . Kitchen Kraft . . . decaled dinnerware lines . . . "go-alongs", the metal, wooden, glass accessories . . . advertising pieces . . .

Post Script:

We never dreamed "The Story of Fiesta" would take so many years to tell—yet here we are, finishing the fourth edition . . . wondering if this is its conclusion. But even if it is, so long as there are those who love these beautiful wares of HLC, there will be no end to its fascination and intrigue!

SUGGESTED VALUES

Values are suggested for items that are in mint condition . . . that is to say, no chips, "chigger bites", or "dings"! Bad glazing and scratches would also reduce the value. The three sager pin marks that are evident on the underside of many pieces are characteristic, and result from the technique employed during the firing process. These should have no adverse effect.

Several dealers, each representing various sections of the country, have contributed their estimates of the value of HLC wares in their areas. From this nationwide sampling, we have compiled an "Olympic" average—that is, we eliminated the highest and the lowest values, and averaged those remaining.

The 50's colors are highly prized and are harder to find, and in most cases have become as desirable as red. For these colors: grey, rose, chartreuse, dark green (and med. green) . . . and of course, any *red* piece, Harlequin and Riviera included, add 25% to the *high* side of the range. Some items may be rarely found in a common color, when possible we will indicate a price for a piece such as this in the listing . . . otherwise, the high side would apply.

Actual measurements may vary as much as ¾" from those listed in the price guide. For instance, the factory lists a dinner plate as 10", when it actually measures 10½". In those instances where actual measurements vary more than ½" from factory sizes we will show actual size in parenthesis.

Color code:
  * made in six original colors; red, dark blue, old ivory, yellow, light green, and turquoise.
  ** made in eleven colors — six original plus rose, grey.
  ** chartreuse, dark green, and medium green.
  *** made in ten colors, no med. green

SUGGESTED VALUES FOR FIESTA

Page 39
Top Row:

(14⅜") 15" Chop plate***	12.00- 15.00
(12¼") Chop plate**	8.00- 12.00

Middle:

11⅝" Compartment plate* (no turquoise)	9.00- 12.00
10½" Compartment plate***	7.00- 10.00

Bottom:

(10½") 10" Dinner plate**	5.00- 8.00
(9½") 9" Luncheon**	3.00- 5.00
(7⅜") 7" Bread and butter**	2.00- 3.00
(6⅜") 6" Dessert plate**	1.50- 2.50

Page 41

8" Deep plate**	9.00- 12.00
Cream soup cup**	9.00- 12.00
(in med. green)	13.00- 17.00
7⅝" Individual salad bowl	18.00- 22.00
6" Dessert bowl**	6.00- 9.00
(in med. green)	18.00- 22.00
4¾" Fruit	4.50- 6.50
(in med. green)	18.00- 22.00
5½" Fruit**	5.00- 7.00

Page 43
Top:

Coffee pot, regular**	28.00- 33.00
Tea cups**	8.00- 12.00
Saucers**	1.00- 2.00

Middle:

Egg cups***	15.00- 18.00

Lower Right:

Tom & Jerry mugs**	15.00- 20.00
(in red)	30.00- 40.00

Page 45
Top:

Disk water pitcher, 2 qt.** 18.00- 22.00
10 oz. tumbler* 15.00- 20.00
Bottom:

Covered sugar** 7.00- 9.00
Creamer, reg.** 4.00- 6.00
Creamer, stick handle* 6.00- 8.50
Utility tray* 8.00- 12.00
Salt and Peppers**, pr. 5.50- 9.00
Page 47
Top:

Oval platter, 12"** 9.00- 13.00
9½" Nappy* 9.00- 12.00
8½" Nappy** 8.00- 10.00
9½" Salad bowl in yellow 22.00- 28.00
     (Unusual color) 40.00- 60.00
Center, Left:

Footed salad bowl* 62.00- 68.00
Bottom, Right:

Fruit bowl, 11¾"* 47.00- 55.00
Page 49
11" Nested bowl, #7* 30.00- 38.00
10" Nested bowl, #6* 20.00- 28.00
9" Nested bowl, #5* 18.50- 25.00
8" Nested bowl, #4* 17.00- 21.00
7" Nested bowl, #3* 14.00- 18.00
6" Nested bowl, #2* 10.00- 13.00
5" Nested bowl, #1* 15.00- 18.50
Any size lid 32.00- 36.00
Center, Left:

Gravy boat** 8.50- 13.00
Bottom, Right:

Casserole** 25.00- 30.00
     (in med. green or 50's colors) 31.00- 38.00
Page 51
Top:

Relish tray* 38.00- 45.00

Comport, 12"* 28.00- 32.00
Bottom:
Coffee Pot, After Dinner* 50.00- 65.00
Coffee cups, A.D.*** 12.00- 15.00
Saucers, A.D.*** 3.50- 5.00
   (red, cup and saucer) 19.00- 24.00
   (50's colors, cup and saucer) 32.00- 40.00
Page 53
Top:
Carafe, 3 pt.* 35.00- 45.00
Ice pitcher, 2 qt.* 18.00- 22.50
Bottom:
2 pt. jug*** 13.50- 17.00
Covered onion soup* 65.00- 78.00
   (in turquoise or red) 88.00-108.00
Page 55
Top:
Ash tray** 12.00- 15.00
Sweets comport* 12.00- 16.00
Mustard* 35.00- 45.00
Marmalade* 47.00- 55.00
Syrup pitcher* 55.00- 67.50
Bottom:
Tea pot, large* 25.00- 30.50
Tea pot, med.** 20.00- 27.00
Page 57
Top:
Vase, 12"* 115.00-140.00
Vase, 10"* 95.00-120.00
Vase, 8"* 72.00- 83.00
Bud vase* 18.00- 23.00
Bottom:
Candleholder, tripod, pr.* 65.00- 75.00
Candleholder, bulb, pr.* 19.00- 24.00
Page 59
Top:
Handled chop plate, 13"* 28.00- 32.00

French casserole (Yellow) 62.00- 78.00
Individual sugar, creamer, tray,
    in yellow and navy blue 44.00- 50.00
Bottom:

Juice pitcher, 30 oz., yellow 6.50- 9.00
    (in red or gray) 31.00- 40.00
Juice tumbler, 5 oz.
    (original six colors and rose) 8.50- 12.00
    (other colors) 21.00- 27.00

Page 61
Metal holders only:
for salt, pepper, mustard 25.00- 30.00
for Kitchen Kraft casserole 7.00- 10.00
for marmalade ....,.... 20.00- 25.00
Fiestawood bowl 30.00- 40.00
3 tier tidbit tray 32.00- 38.00
Serenade juice set,
    30 oz. pitcher 28.00- 35.00
    5 oz. tumbler 18.00- 22.00

Page 63
Metal holders only:
for 9½″ nappy 6.00- 8.00
for cream soup, jam set 20.00- 25.00
for juice set 12.00- 17.00
Tea pot, with metal dripolator insert,
    complete unit 35.00- 45.00
Sta-brite stainless flatware with colored plastic handles
    3 pc. place setting 5.00- 6.50
Fiestawood Lazy Suzan, 20″ 34.00- 42.00

Page 65
Top:

Metal holder only,
for jug and tumblers 25.00- 30.00
Bottom:

Metal holder only,
for mustard and marmalade 35.00- 40.00
Decorated relish tray 50.00- 60.00
Tablecloth and napkins 25.00- 30.00

Page 67
Top:

Pine Cone teapot, med.	17.00- 22.00
Fiestawood hors d'oeuvre tray	35.00- 45.00
KK covered jar with decal/lid	45.00- 55.00

Bottom, Left:

Boudoir lamp	50.00- 75.00

Bottom, Right:

Fiesta lamp base, fabricated body of any type	50.00- 75.00

Page 69
Top:

Tom & Jerry bowl	53.00- 62.00
Tom & Jerry mugs	21.00- 25.00

Middle:

Advertising mugs, ea.	15.00- 18.00
(blanks)	11.00- 13.00

Bottom:

7″ Plate	1.00- 2.00
9″ Plate	1.00- 2.00
10″ Plate	1.00- 2.00

Page 71
Top:

Tall mug, hotel china	7.00- 10.00
Sit 'N Sip carton only	5.00- 7.00
Tall mug, with advertising	9.00- 12.00
Nursery mug	17.00- 20.00
Sit 'N Sip sets	21.00- 26.00
Advertising mug in Fiesta color	19.00- 21.00

Bottom:

Advertising mug, color inside	14.00- 17.00
Mug with Antique Car decal	18.00- 25.00
Mug with color inside, blank	12.00- 14.00

Page 73
Top:

15″ Chop plate with decal	28.50- 33.50
Tom & Jerry mug	4.00- 5.00
Tom & Jerry bowl	12.00- 16.00

Bottom:

Fiestawood tray, 16½″	27.00- 35.00
Advertising ash tray	25.00- 30.00

Metal base only 15.00- 20.00
Wooden handle only 5.00- 7.50
Page 75
Top:
5" Fruit (Lazarus) 10.00- 15.00
Egg cup (Lazarus) 20.00- 25.00
Middle:
15" Chop plate with floral decal 25.00- 35.00
7" Plate with floral decal 5.00- 10.00
13" Chop plate with turkey decal 35.00- 50.00
Bottom:
Calendar plate, 1954, 10" 14.00- 18.00
"Good Luck", 1955, 9" 26.00- 30.00
Calendar plate, 1955, 10" 18.00- 24.00
Page 77
Top:
Plate with floral decal, 10" 10.00- 12.50
Tea cup with floral decal 9.00- 12.00
Saucer with floral decal 4.00- 6.00
Fruit with floral decal, 4¾" 5.50- 7.00
Bottom, Left:
Footed salad bowl with decal 65.00- 75.00
Bottom, Right:
Cake plate, 10" 42.50- 55.00
Page 79
Top row:
Creamer, experimental, 4" 20.00- 27.00
Comport, 10" × 2½", rare 65.00- 90.00
Individual tea pot, with cover, experimental 75.00-100.00
Bottom:
Individual red creamer 28.00- 32.00
(in turquoise) 45.00- 60.00
Individual turquoise tray 45.00- 60.00
(in yellow) 55.00- 70.00
Medium Green fruit, 4¾" 20.00- 26.00
Relish section, experimental 30.00- 40.00
Original Fiesta carton 8.00- 10.00

Page 81
Upper Left:
    Decaled Fruit Comport 30.00- 40.00
Center Right:
    Decaled Relish 45.00- 55.00
Center Left:
    8 pc. Cake set 25.00- 30.00
Bottom Right:
    Bicentennial bowl 15.00- 20.00
        mug 15.00- 20.00
Page 83
Top:
    Bread box 25.00- 35.00
    Garbage can 25.00- 35.00
Bottom:
    Canister set 26.00- 32.50
    Napkin holder 12.00- 18.00
Page 85
Top:
    Saturday Evening Post, intact 15.00- 20.00
    Fiesta price listing, 1965 .... 3.00- 5.00
    Fiesta price listing, 1939 .... 9.00- 12.50
    Menu, any size 5.00- 7.00
    Sheet of decals 15.00- 25.00
    Corn package 5.00- 7.00
Page 87
Top:
    Handscraft egg cooker, complete set
       (with egg cups as shown, and tray) 47.50- 60.00
       (cooker only) 30.00- 40.00
       (egg cups, as shown) 7.00- 9.00
Bottom:
    Footed cake stand 30.00- 35.00

FIESTA CASUALS
Values apply to both patterns.
Page 89
    Oval platter 15.00- 20.00

10″ Plate	7.00-	9.00
7″ Plate	5.50-	7.00
Saucer	4.00-	6.00

AMBERSTONE

Page 91

Dinner plate	3.50-	5.00
Dessert dish	1.50-	3.00
Bread and Butter	2.00-	2.50
Coffee cup with saucer	6.00-	8.00
Vegetable bowl	4.50-	5.50
Covered sugar	4.00-	6.00
Creamer	3.00-	4.50
Oval platter	6.00-	8.00
Large soup plate	4.00-	5.00
Ash tray	12.00-	16.00
Salt and pepper, pr.	8.00-	10.00
Salad plate	1.50-	2.50
Soup cereal	2.00-	3.00
Covered casserole	15.00-	17.00
Sauce boat	10.00-	12.00
Relish tray	10.00-	12.00
Coffee server	18.00-	22.00
Tea server	12.00-	14.00
Covered butter	24.00-	28.00
Round serving platter	12.00-	14.00
Jumbo salad bowl	6.00-	8.00
Covered jam jar	20.00-	24.00
Serving pitcher, disk	14.00-	20.00
Jumbo mug	4.00-	6.00
Pie plate	20.00-	24.00

CASUALSTONE

Items in plain Antique Gold are priced with Ironstone, since they are interchangeable.

Page 93

Oval platter/gold design	9.00-	12.00
10″ Plate/gold design	4.00-	5.00
Saucer/gold design	1.50-	2.50

FIESTA IRONSTONE

Prices apply to Antique Gold, Turf Green, and all restyled items in red.

Page 95

Med. tea pot	8.50- 11.00
13" Oval platter	5.00- 6.00
Coffee server	10.00- 14.00
10" Dinner plate	2.50- 3.50
Disk water pitcher	2.50- 3.00
Sugar/cover	2.00- 3.50
Creamer	3.00- 4.00
Marmalade	16.00- 22.00
Large nappy	5.00- 6.00
Small fruit	2.50- 3.50
Salad bowl	7.00- 9.00
Tea cups	3.00- 4.00
Saucer	.75- 1.00
Sauceboat	4.50- 5.50
Sauceboat stand	9.00- 12.00
(in red)	30.00- 35.00
7" Plate	1.00- 2.00
Coffee mug	4.00- 5.50
Covered casserole	10.00- 12.00
Shakers, pr.	4.00- 5.00
Ash tray	3.00- 5.00

FIESTA KITCHEN KRAFT

Page 99

Covered refrigerator jars, mixed colors	45.00- 55.00
Covered jug, either size	65.00- 75.00

Page 101

Top:

Casserole, 8½"	30.00- 40.00
Casserole, 7½"	30.00- 40.00
Individual casserole	35.00- 45.00

Middle:

Large covered jar	65.00- 78.00
Med. covered jar	62.00- 75.00
Small covered jar	63.00- 76.00

Bottom:

10″ mixing bowl	29.00-	35.00
8″ mixing bowl	25.00-	32.00
6″ mixing bowl	16.00-	18.00

Page 103
Top:

Cake plate	17.00-	22.00
Pie plate, 10″	20.00-	25.00
Pie plate, 9″	20.00-	27.00

Middle:

Metal holders only:

for 10″ pie plate	9.00-	13.00
for casserole	6.00-	10.00
for platter	13.50-	16.50
Oval platter only, 13″	30.00-	40.00

Bottom:

Spoon	23.00-	30.00
Fork	25.00-	32.00
Server	26.00-	35.00
Salt and peppers, pr.	27.00-	37.00

HARLEQUIN

Page 109
Top:

10″ Plate	3.00-	4.00
9″ Plate	2.00-	3.00
7″ Plate	1.00-	2.00
6″ Plate	.75-	1.00

Center:

13″ Platter	4.50-	6.50
11″ Platter	3.50-	5.50

Center:

Deep plate	3.00-	5.00
36's Oatmeal, 6½″	2.50-	4.00
5½″ Fruit	1.50-	3.00
Cream soup	3.50-	5.50

Page 111
    9" Nappy ., ...   3.00- 5.00
    36's Bowl 4.00- 5.50
    Casserole with lid 15.00- 20.00
    9" Oval baker 3.50- 5.50
    Individual salad bowl, 7" 4.00- 6.00
Page 113
Top:
    Service water jug 9.00- 14.00
    Water tumbler 8.00- 12.00
Bottom:
    Tea pot 10.00- 15.00
    Tea cups 3.00- 4.50
    Saucer 50-   .75
Page 115
Top:
    Covered sugar 3.00- 5.00
    Creamer, regular 2.50- 4.00
    Creamer with high lip 15.00- 18.00
    Salt and peppers, pr. 3.50- 5.00
    Marmalade 27.50- 37.50
    Novelty creamer 4.00- 6.00
Bottom:
    Sauceboat 4.00- 6.00
    Tumbler with car decal 10.00- 16.00
    22 oz. Jug 7.00- 11.00
       (in grey, chartreuse, dk. gr., med. gr.)   12.00- 18.00
Page 117
Top:
    Saucer/ash tray 16.00- 20.00
    Nut dish, 3" 4.00- 5.50
    Syrup 45.00- 55.00
    Large cup, tankard 23.00- 30.00
    Ash tray, reg. 14.00- 18.00
    Ash tray, basketweave 18.00- 22.00
    Covered butter 25.00- 32.00
    Perfume bottle 20.00- 25.00

Bottom:

5 pc. Relish tray	30.00- 35.00
Nut dish	16.00- 20.00

Page 119
Top:

Candleholders, pr.	28.00- 32.00
Double egg cup	4.00- 6.00
Individual egg cup	8.00- 12.00
Coffee cup, After Dinner	6.00- 10.00
(in 50's colors)	10.00- 15.00
Saucer, A.D.	3.00- 4.50
(in 50's colors)	6.00- 7.00

Bottom:

Spoon rest, in Harlequin colors	70.00- 80.00
(in 50's colors and red)	100.00-125.00
(with original label)	110.00-125.00
(in 50's colors, with label)	140.00-175.00
Advertising spoon rest	50.00- 65.00
(white, no lettering)	40.00- 50.00

Page 121
Top:

Metal holder and tumbler	7.00- 10.00
Donkey with salt and peppers	5.00- 10.00
Individual creamer	4.00- 6.00

Bottom:

Large tankard with saucer, set	27.50- 35.00
Lamp base	50.00- 75.00
Harlequin pamphlet	7.00- 12.00

HARLEQUIN ANIMALS

Page 123
Top:

Harlequin animals	32.00- 40.00

Bottom:

Mavericks	15.00- 25.00

RIVIERA

Page 127
Top:

10″ Plate	4.50- 6.50
9″ Plate	3.00- 4.00

7" Plate	1.50-	2.50
6" Plate	1.00-	1.50
Center:		
11½" Platter, oval well	5.00-	6.00
11¼" Platter, with handles	5.50-	6.50
Bottom:		
13" Platter with handles	7.00-	9.00
12" Platter with handles	7.00-	9.00
Page 129		
Top:		
Tea pot	17.00-	22.00
Tea cup	4.00-	5.00
Saucer	1.00-	2.00
Bottom:		
5½" Fruit	1.50-	3.00
9¼" Oval baker	4.00-	5.50
Deep plate	3.00-	5.00
9" Oval baker	3.00-	5.00
8¼" Nappy	4.00-	5.50
Page 131		
Top:		
Juice jug, yellow	25.00-	35.00
(in mauve blue)	60.00-	85.00
Juice tumbler	16.00-	20.00
Center, Left:		
Sauceboat	4.00-	6.00
Bottom, Right:		
Casserole with lid	18.00-	23.00
Page 133		
Handled tumblers	15.00-	20.00
Covered jug	25.00-	35.00
Quarter lb. butter, cover	25.00-	32.00
Covered syrup	22.00-	30.00
Salt and peppers, pr.	4.00-	5.00
One half lb. butter, cover	24.00-	30.00
Creamer, reg.	3.00-	4.00
Covered sugar	4.00-	5.00

Page 135
Top:

Complete batter set 55.00- 70.00

Bottom:

Tumblers 3.00- 4.50
Riviera pamphlet 8.00- 11.00
Demitasse cup and saucer 12.00- 16.00

CHILD'S SETS

Page 137
Top:

Dick Tracy Child's Set
Mug 25.00- 30.00
Bowl, 5½″ 25.00- 30.00
Plate, 7″ 15.00- 20.00
Original box 10.00- 15.00

Bottom:

Animal Characters Child's Set .... (same as above)

Page 139
Top:

Tom Thumb and the Butterfly Child's Set   (same as above)
Bottom:
Child's Western dinnerware
Cup and Saucer 15.00- 20.00
Plate, 9″ 8.00- 12.00
Fruit, 5″ 8.00- 12.00

DECALED CENTURY

Page 141
Top:

9″ Plate, Old English scene 2.50- 4.00
9″ Plate, Columbine 2.50- 4.00
9″ Plate, Briar Rose 2.50- 3.00

Center:

13″ Platter, gold decal 3.00- 4.00
11″ Platter, Petipoint 3.00- 4.00

Bottom:

12″ Advertising platter 8.00- 10.00
15½″ Platter/square well 10.00- 12.00
10½″ Platter/oval well 5.00- 8.00

VIRGINIA ROSE

Page 143

Top:

11½" Platter	3.50-	5.00
10½" Dinner plate	3.00-	4.00
10½" Platter	2.50-	3.00
8½" Vegetable bowl	2.50-	3.50
9" Plate	2.50-	3.00
10½" Covered casserole	12.00-	18.00
7½" Vegetable bowl	2.00-	3.00
9½" Platter	3.00-	4.00
8" Plate	2.00-	3.00
Deep Plate	3.50-	4.00

Bottom:

7" Plate	1.50-	2.50
5" Milk pitcher	6.00-	8.50
Double egg cup	3.50-	5.00
6" Plate	1.00-	1.50
Sauceboat	4.00-	6.00
½ lb. butter dish	20.00-	25.00
Covered sugar	4.00-	5.00
Creamer	3.00-	4.00
Mug	6.00-	8.50
Deep bowl	3.00-	4.00

Page 145

Top:

11½" Platter	3.50-	5.00
15½" Platter	4.00-	6.00
Nested bowl, large	10.00-	12.00
Nested bowl, med.	8.00-	10.00
Nested bowl, small	6.00-	8.00
KK casserole	9.00-	14.00
9½" Pie Plate	8.00-	10.00
8" Oval vegetable	2.50-	3.50
5" Fruit	1.50-	2.50
9" Vegetable	3.00-	4.00
Salt and Pepper, pr.	3.00-	4.00
Cup and Saucer	3.50-	4.50
6" Oatmeal	2.00-	3.00

Bottom:
Nested bowl set, 5", 6", 7", 8", 9½" 20.00- 25.00

RHYTHM ROSE

Page 147

Top:

9" Dinner plate	2.50- 3.00
10½" Cake plate	5.00- 7.00
9" KK underplate	6.00- 10.00
KK jug pitcher	8.00- 10.00
8" Deep plate	3.50- 4.00
8½" KK casserole	8.00- 14.00
A.D. cup and saucer	6.00- 8.00
9½" KK pie plate	8.00- 10.00
Sauceboat	4.00- 6.00
Cake Server	6.00- 8.00

Bottom:

6" Plate	1.00- 1.50
KK coffee pot	12.00- 20.00
Nested bowl, large	10.00- 12.00
Nested bowl, med.	8.00- 10.00
Nested bowl, small	6.00- 8.00
KK coffee pot	12.00- 20.00
6" KK underplate	5.00- 8.00
Tea Pot	12.00- 20.00
13" Platter	4.00- 6.00
Covered sugar	4.00- 5.00
Creamer	3.00- 4.00

PRISCILLA PATTERN DINNERWARE

Page 149

Coffee pot	18.00- 23.00
Fruit bowl, 9½"	8.00- 12.00
Sugar	4.50- 7.00
Creamer	4.00- 5.00
Gravy boat	5.50- 7.00
Cup and saucer	4.00- 5.50
Oval vegetable, 9"	3.50- 5.00
Soup, 8½"	3.50- 5.00
Platter, 13½"	4.50- 6.50

Dinner plate, 9″	3.50-	5.00
Luncheon plate, 8″	2.50-	3.50
Dessert plate, 6″	1.50-	2.50
Fruit, 5″	2.00-	3.00

DOGWOOD

Bottom:

Plate, 9″	2.50-	3.50
Fruit, 5½″	2.50-	3.00
Dessert plate, 6½″	1.50-	2.50

SERENADE

Page 151

Top:

Chop plate, 13″	5.00-	6.50
Dinner plate, 9″	3.00-	4.00
Bread and butter plate, 7″	2.00-	2.50
Cup and Saucer	4.00-	5.00
Fruit, 6″	2.50-	3.50
Shakers, pr.	5.00-	7.00
Vegetable bowl, 9″	4.00-	5.00
Casserole, with lid	9.00-	15.00
Serenade KK casserole with lid	9.00-	15.00

JUBILEE

Bottom:

Plate, 10″, calendar	4.00-	7.00
Jubilee pamphlet	6.00-	8.00

TANGO

Page 153

Top:

Egg cups	4.00-	5.00
Cup and saucer	4.00-	5.00
Dessert plate, 6″	1.50-	2.00
Shakers, pr.	3.00-	4.50
Deep soup	2.50-	3.50

RHYTHM

Bottom:

Plate, 9″	3.00-	4.00
Cup and saucer	3.50-	5.00
Dessert plate, 6″	1.50-	2.50
Fruit, 5½″	1.50-	2.50

MEXICANA

Page 155
Top:

36's oatmeal, 6″	4.00-	5.50
Fruit, 5½″	2.50-	4.50
Glass tumblers, ea.	7.00-	10.00
Tea cup	5.00-	6.50
Saucer	1.00-	1.50
Deep plate	4.00-	5.50
Plate, 9″	2.50-	4.00

Bottom:

10″ Plate	4.00-	5.00
13″ Platter	4.00-	8.00
9″ Plate	2.50-	4.00
Sauceboat	5.00-	8.00
9″ Oval Vegetable	5.00-	7.50
Cup and Saucer	6.00-	8.00
Sauceboat liner	6.00-	9.00
Covered sugar	4.00-	6.00
Creamer	3.00-	4.00

Page 157
Top:

8″ Deep	2.50-	4.00
11″ Platter	3.50-	6.50
7″ Plate	1.50-	2.50
6″ Oatmeal	4.00-	6.00
8″ Vegetable bowl	5.00-	6.50
6″ Plate	1.00-	2.00
5″ Nappy	3.00-	4.50
4¾″ lug soup	5.00-	8.00

MEXICANA YELLOWSTONE

Bottom:

11½″ Platter	3.50-	6.50
13½″ Platter	4.00-	8.00
10″ Platter	3.00-	6.00
Creamer	3.00-	4.00
Egg cup	8.00-	10.00
Sugar	4.00-	6.00
Egg cup, rolled edge	10.00-	15.00
8½″ Casserole/lid	17.50-	20.00
Tri-pod candleholders, pr.	40.00-	50.00
8½″ Sauceboat liner	6.00-	9.00

Page 159
Top:

6″ Plate	1.00- 2.00
7″ Plate	1.50- 2.50
Sauceboat	5.00- 8.00
4½″ Lug soup	5.00- 8.00
8½″ Vegetable bowl	5.00- 6.50
Cup and saucer	6.00- 8.00

Bottom:

9″ Plate	2.50- 4.00
9½″ Plate	3.50- 5.00
6″ Plate	1.00- 2.00
9½″ Vegetable bowl	5.00- 7.50
8″ Deep plate	4.00- 5.50
6″ Oatmeal	4.00- 6.00
½ lb. butter with cover	28.00- 40.00
5″ Fruit	3.00- 4.50

HACIENDA

Page 161
Top:

9″ Plate	2.50- 3.50
11″ Platter with square well	6.00- 8.00
6″ Plate	1.00- 2.00
Creamer	3.00- 4.00
Covered sugar	4.00- 5.50
Tea pot with lid	18.00- 22.00
Sauceboat	5.00- 8.00
Cup and saucer	6.00- 8.00
5″ Fruit	3.00- 4.00

Bottom:

11½″ Platter with oval well	6.00- 8.00
13½″ Platter with oval well	7.50- 10.00
8″ Deep plate	4.00- 5.00
8″ Vegetable bowl	5.00- 7.00
10″ Dinner plate	4.00- 5.00

9″ Vegetable bowl	5.00-	7.50
8″ Casserole, Natulis shape	20.00-	27.50
6″ Oatmeal	4.00-	5.50

Page 163

Tablecloth and napkins	23.00-	28.00
Tumblers, either style	3.00-	5.00
Cup and saucer	7.00-	10.00

CONCHITA

Center:

11½″ Platter	3.50-	6.50
13½″ Platter	4.00-	8.00
8″ Deep plate	4.00-	5.00
5″ Dessert	3.00-	4.00
9″ Plate	2.50-	4.00
8″ Vegetable	5.00-	6.50
Covered sugar	4.00-	6.00
Creamer	3.00-	4.00
Cup and Saucer	7.00-	8.00

KITCHEN KRAFT AND OVEN SERVE

Bottom:

Large Covered jar	45.00-	55.00
Large Mixing bowl	16.00-	18.00
Medium Covered jar	40.00-	55.00
Covered jug	60.00-	75.00
10½″ Cake plate	13.00-	18.00
8″ Casserole	24.00-	30.00
9″ Underplate	10.00-	15.00

Page 165

Top:

10″ Pie plate	16.00-	18.00
10″ Mixing bowl	18.00-	20.00
Spoon	18.00-	20.00
Pie server	18.00-	20.00
Fork	18.00-	20.00
8½″ Casserole	24.00-	30.00
Salt and Pepper, pr.	22.00-	24.00

Bottom:

Large covered jar	45.00- 55.00
10½″ Cake plate	13.00- 18.00
Covered jug	60.00- 75.00
Salt and peppers, pr.	22.00- 24.00
Refrigerator jar, unit	8.00- 12.00
Lid	20.00- 25.00

Page 167

Top:

Medium Covered jar	24.00- 28.00
Small Covered jar	24.00- 28.00
Large Covered jar	24.00- 28.00
Refrigerator unit, ea.	6.00- 8.00
Lid	8.00- 10.00
Covered jug	18.00- 24.00
Individual casserole with lid	18.00- 22.00

Bottom:

Large Covered jar	24.00- 28.00
10½″ Cake plate	13.00- 18.00
Large Nested bowl	10.00- 15.00
Medium Nested bowl	8.00- 12.00
Small Nested bowl	7.00- 10.00
Medium Jar	24.00- 28.00
14½″ Fruit bowl	35.00- 45.00
8½″ Casserole in metal holder	12.00- 15.00
Small Covered jar	24.00- 28.00
Cake server	10.00- 12.00
9½″ Pie plate	8.00- 10.00
Salt and Pepper, pr.	12.00- 15.00

Page 169

Top:

10″ Mixing bowl	6.00- 8.00
Server	7.00- 9.00
Pie plate, 10″	8.00- 10.00

Bottom:

7″ Nappy	2.00- 3.50
8½″ Casserole	5.50- 7.50
6″ Mixing bowl	2.50- 3.50
8″ Oval baker	2.50- 3.50

9″ Plate	2.00-	3.50
Custard cup	1.50-	2.50
Fruit, 5¾″	1.50-	2.50

Page 171
Top:

10″ Pie plate/Tulips	8.00-	10.00
10″ Pie plate/Wild Rose	8.00-	10.00
10″ Pie plate/floral	8.00-	10.00

Middle:

10″ Pie plate/Kitchen Bouquet	8.00-	10.00
13″ Platter/Kitchen Bouquet	8.00-	10.00

Bottom:

Cake plate/floral	8.00-	10.00
11″ Pie plate	8.00-	10.00
Server	7.00-	9.00

THE AMERICAN POTTER

Page 173
Top:

HLC World's Fair plate, '39 or '40	28.00-	35.00

Bottom:

Cake set	20.00-	23.00
Bowl	17.00-	23.00
Plate	20.00-	23.00
Marmalade and cover	18.00-	22.00
Pitcher	22.00-	26.00

Page 175
Top:

Potter's Plate	16.00-	19.00
Original box	14.00-	17.50
Zodiac cup and saucer	31.00-	37.50

Bottom:

Green vase, 5½″	17.00-	21.00
Turquoise vase, 7″	21.00-	25.00
Yellow, 4½″	17.00-	20.00
Small vase, any size	15.00-	19.00
Bowl	10.00-	14.00
Candleholder, 2″	17.00-	21.00
Individual creamer	17.00-	20.00

Page 177

INDEX